STOCK MARKET BLUEPRINTS

by

EDWARD S. JENSEN

Quick & Reilly, Inc.
Members New York Stock Exchange
120 Wall Street, New York, N.Y. 10005

Stock Market Blueprints

LIBRARY OF CONGRESS CATALOG CARD NUMBER: 67-20512

Printed in the United States of America

FIRST EDITION 1967
SECOND EDITION 1969
THIRD EDITION 1977
FOURTH EDITION 1981
FIFTH EDITION 1983
SIXTH EDITION 1984

FOREWORD

In May of 1975 Quick & Reilly, Inc. became the first New York Stock Exchange member firm to offer substantial commission discounts to all investors. Since the majority of our clients make their own investment decisions, we felt that STOCK MARKET BLUEPRINTS might be of assistance to them in understanding the movement of the market, as well as in selecting stocks to buy and sell.

Over the years we have found that Mr. Jensen's guidelines for success in the stock market are proven and timeless.

It is our sincere hope that you, too, will find them helpful.

LESLIE C. QUICK, JR.
President
Quick & Reilly, Inc.

May, 1977

PREFACE

During my years of stock market activities, I have witnessed thousands of dollars being spent on advertising and publications by brokerage firms, the New York Stock Exchange, and the National Association of Securities Dealers advising investors to "investigate before you invest" and to "know your objectives." This would certainly seem the logical thing for investors to do and where no confusion should arise. Stop before reading further and ask yourself this question: "What is my objective in buying stocks?" I'll bet that the first answer that popped into your mind went something like this: "All I want to do is to make money."

Relax, you're normal. This is the exact answer that the majority of investors have given me. But think for a moment about the various types of stocks that we have to select from in order to *make money*. Some of the stocks are those of the largest companies in the world. Some are those of smaller but more profitably operated companies. Some will be those of infants that may someday be giants. And still other stocks may be those of companies in a declining phase and, unless new products or services are found to alter this trend, they may in fact be bankrupt within a few years.

To establish a clear definition of one's investment objectives, it becomes necessary to answer the following questions: How much risk am I willing to assume? How much appreciation do I desire? How soon do I expect to realize these profits? If these three questions involving RISK, POTENTIAL and TIME can be specifically answered, then you are a long way toward your goal of making money.

However, now the problem begins. In the investment books and publications I have read, there has been little or no attempt to define investment objectives in the above terms. Phrases such as "businessman's risk," "conservative investor" and "speculator" are glibly tossed around without any concrete meaning attached to them. I have looked at lists of stocks which supposedly had "speculative" appeal and yet some of these issues were, in my opinion, blue chips and rather "conservative."

The primary task of the pages ahead is to establish some solid definitions and plans that may help clear up some of the confusion that exists. Remember, along with one's health and family, money is very dear to most of us and it is assumed that prudence and care should be exercised in the management of this money.

Investing one's money successfully is no different than any other profitable venture; it requires *planning*. Planning is the logical step-by-step process wherein you first define the goals desired and the problems that must be overcome in order to accomplish this goal. Secondly, you must examine all possible solutions and finally arrive at a conclusion based on the best available evidence at the time. Should the conclusion prove incorrect, other solutions may be attempted until success is attained.

This book is written in two parts. Part I, The Foundation, defines the total investment problem and lays down the ground rules which the author thinks are most likely to maximize success. Part II, The Blueprints, puts forth various plans that are designed to meet the objectives and emotional temperament of the individual investor.

TABLE OF CONTENTS

PART I. THE FOUNDATION

TABLE OF CONTENTS
(Continued)

PART II. THE BLUEPRINTS

ILLUSTRATIONS

THE FOUNDATION

*"I believe the true road to pre-
eminent success in any line is to
make yourself master of that line."*

Andrew Carnegie

Chapter I

STOCK MARKET LOGIC

Before you start to define your goal and select a blueprint, it becomes essential that you lay a solid foundation on which to build. This book is not written for beginners and it is assumed that you have general knowledge and familiarization with such questions as: What is a stock? What is a bond? What is the function and operation of the New York Stock Exchange? What is the Dow Jones Industrial Average or the Standard & Poor's Average? What is meant by volume? What is a short sale? What is the function and operation of the Over-the-Counter Market? These must have a clear and specific meaning to you before you read further. As there are many books covering in ample fashion these basics, it will be my purpose to put your thinking straight on points where most often confusion arises because a true understanding of the fundamentals is clouded or forgotten.

As an example, if asked the question, "What makes stock prices move up or down?" what would your immediate answer be? There is only one *true* answer and that is that at any given moment there exists a greater demand for a certain stock than there is supply at a specific price level. Then the price moves up. The opposite, of course, is a greater supply than demand at a specific price level, which drives the price lower. This phenomenon is called the supply-demand factor, and explains how the auction markets of the listed exchanges and the Over-the-

1

Counter Market — with slight variation — operate. Supply-demand considerations are the only true answer for why stock prices move up or down. This is true day to day, month to month, year to year, and will be as long as our markets function in a free auction system.

If you started to answer this question by reference to earnings, products, management, or dividends, you were jumping to one of several possible reasons that may *create* excess supply or demand, not the actual cause itself.

I have talked with many, so-called knowledgeable and experienced investors, who do not clearly understand the full implication of the supply-demand factor. These investors are completely baffled when—upon reading a piece of bad news about a company—the price moves up. Or, on the other hand, when they read a glowing report on the company, they find the price of the stock moving down. This is because they have not learned another important, though often confusing, fundamental, which is: Stocks move in *anticipation* of good or bad news.

Anticipation of a new product, new contract, higher earnings or dividends, is a far greater motivating force than the fact in itself. This has given rise to the stock market adage "buy rumor, sell news," and certainly while this is not an ironclad rule, it does have about a 75% batting average on a short term basis.

This brings us to our third important fundamental which is that all factors, laws, rules or guidelines mentioned or laid down in this book are based on a probability factor that is approximately correct. To the best of my knowledge there is no such thing as a perfect system, a perfect rule or formula. All attempts are an effort to establish a probability factor hopefully greater than 50%. If it doesn't work more than 50% of the time, it isn't worth discussing. Most of the ideas stressed in this book have, in the opinion of the author, a 65% probability factor or better, unless otherwise noted.

By now there should be several unanswered questions lurking in your mind about our first three fundamentals which all add up to something like, WHY?

Starting with fundamental number one—supply-demand—it should be obvious that the fact that the stock is moving higher or lower is much more important than the exact reason why, which is usually not immediately available to you as a private investor. Remember, you are in the big league, and for every buyer there must be a seller, so let's be logical: if you knew for sure or with a high probability factor that a company in which you own a large block of stock was in serious financial trouble, which may even mean bankruptcy for the company, would you go tell all of your friends and associates, who also own shares, *before* you sold your block of shares? If you would, you're a born loser and this book will be of little value to you. A rational, logical man, acting in his own best interest, is likely to quietly and quickly sell off his shares.

Looking at it the other way around: assuming that you know a company has perfected a revolutionary new product that is likely to add substantially to its profitability over the immediate period ahead, the logical man quietly and steadily begins to buy.

The question you may be asking is, "How come I don't get clued in on these grand new products?" The answer is you are probably not doing enough *work* to uncover these new ideas and products. Secondly, the most common reason is the inability of most people to recognize the future potential or trend towards these new products. For example, the Volkswagen has become one of the largest selling autos in the U.S., but most people had a good belly laugh when they first saw one.

If only one man (in actual practice, obviously several) has knowledge of some new development that leads him to want to buy a certain stock, then he must find other people who will sell at the price he is willing to pay. Now people sell for many reasons that are not necessarily sound investment reasons: the need for cash may arise from thousands of different personal factors, e.g., illness, a greater desire to own a new boat or car, settlement of an estate to pay taxes, etc.

A knowledgeable large investor who is quietly buying will, for a time, not disturb the price movement of a stock very much. But his buying, along with others also persistently buying, will eventually absorb all the ready supply in a particular price zone. Then the price begins to move upward until someone else decides to sell, and thus an upward price trend begins. The first sign of any upward price movement in a stock is likely to be detected by only the most astute analysts. They in turn begin to do a rundown on the company and industry.

Now these early analysts, *without* any specific knowledge or reason, but knowing that stocks move in anticipation of change, may begin buying, perhaps only small amounts at first. Thus the price moves higher and catches the attention of others who will also conduct their investigations.

The vast majority of money made in the stock market is made on anticipation of change and not by being able to pinpoint one specific reason, yet the vast majority of investors desire a specific reason before committing their funds. It might be assumed that the president or directors of a company are certainly in a position to pinpoint why they think their stock should do well, but in practice this is not always the case. First, most executives will attempt to be extremely fair about the forecast for their company. Thus, an announcement of improvement is usually prefaced by telling of all the obstacles that must be surmounted in order to make improvement possible. Such remarks as "if," "hopefully," "contingent upon," etc., leave you as a prospective investor anything but optimistic about the whole situation. But *change* for the better is where money is made, and a clear understanding that price is unlikely to move higher unless rational men anticipate some definite change for the better, is paramount to understanding and making money in a free auction market.

Finally, it may be asked why there is no perfect solution or answer to the investment problem. We are not dealing strictly with balance sheets. If you have learned the lesson of these last few paragraphs, it should be obvious that we are dealing with what people *think*. Present all known facts to ten different investors and they will find ten different reasons why they will or will not buy that specific company.

One final thought must be added to any discussion of the supply and demand factor in the stock market and that is the distinction between mass money—those who generally win—and mass people—those who generally lose. It is said that all you have to do to make money in the stock market is to "Buy low and sell high." No truer words have ever been written, but very few people have actually thought beyond these words as to what factors about the company or industry are present when the price is low. Obviously, you are very unlikely to find the kind of good news that makes the stock irresistible to buy. Quite the contrary. In order for prices to be low the news you read and hear is apt to be bad, disappointing or uncertain.

It should be obvious then that it is going to take a tough investor to overcome these psychological barriers, and yet that is exactly what must be done in order to make money. Mass money needs time to acquire any sizable position in a particular industry or stock. That is why most stocks typically fall rapidly in price for several months and then begin to generally move sideways for a year or longer before again making any significant price advance. It is during this sideways movement that all the reasons for the big drop in price are revealed, and with each dose of bad news (such as lesser earnings, loss of contracts, product failures, foreign competition, dividend reduction, etc.) more and more investors become discouraged and sell their stock. Who is doing the buying? Those who are selling are the ones who needed a specific reason, and as the stock dropped from $100 down to $40 were completely baffled when no specific reasons were forthcoming.

But now, as the stock begins to move sideways in a relatively narrow range, e.g., $35 to $45, they find out all these bad reasons and they will typically sell, maybe in disgust, possibly for a tax loss, and most certainly if they can ever "get out even." Again, if there is a buyer for every seller, who in his right mind would be buying when the news is so black? The answer is mass money. (A word of caution: my references here are to established companies in basic industries that have intrinsic value, not to some promoter's pipedream.)

To put it more bluntly, *mass money absolutely needs bad news and discouraging events to get mass people to sell their stocks.* Now it should not require a Ph.D. degree to figure out what conditions must be necessary when mass money wants to sell their holdings. Using the above example, let's say after a year of sideways price movement in the $35 to $45 area, the stock begins to move up again, and two years later we find the price pushing $150 per share. The facts then show the company didn't go bankrupt, but perhaps a new president was brought in, who cut costs, stepped up promotion efforts, and now has the earnings in a straight upward trend and it looks like the sky is the limit. I assume you get the picture. Every emotion makes you want to buy and certainly the news is nothing but good.

If things are that good, then what rational man would sell his stock? *Mass money who bought some time earlier must have good news and events in order to find buyers for their stock.* Mass money is more likely to buy closer to the bottom than to sell right on the top. Since stocks come down generally faster than they go up, mass money will usually begin selling before the final top is reached and will keep selling even into the early stages of the next major downtrend.

Does this view of the basics of how major money is made in the stock market preclude you as a possibly successful smaller investor? Most assuredly not, but you had better re-read the above paragraphs to be sure that there is no confusion in your mind as to how the game is played. All that is necessary is to join forces with the big boys and be sure not to be a hog about getting the absolute top.

Understanding the preceding paragraphs should make you begin to harden your emotions and help you in the development of "stock market logic." Starting with the premise that a logical investor will at all times act in a logical manner, in his own self-interest, is what makes the difference between a cool, calculated investment and a guessing game of chance. Yet some of the most logical people and some of the most successful business-men are the poorest investors. Why?

A good engineer building a bridge should be able to calculate accurately the structural requirements, and with a little more arithmetic he should be able to determine precisely how much it will cost and how long a construction period is neces-sary. If he's really good, and it is his money and reputation at stake (contrary to government employees), he will calculate for every conceivable contingency he can think of, such as material price hikes, labor problems or weather delays, etc. I have stated that this engineer was successful and as such he covered every possible base before attempting to even start this project.

This same man, however, is likely to read a glowing report about a company in the local paper. He calls a broker and buys the issue. He will ask the broker if XYZ Company is a good company. What is the broker likely to say? The broker is in the business of buying and selling stocks. He knows that when you ask that question you are already two-thirds sold on buying. Do you expect him to say, "No, it's a terrible company and you are an idiot to consider it"? Quite the contrary. He read the article too, so all he has to say is that it "sounds good" and you buy the stock.

Taking the example of a doctor who has performed hun-dreds of appendectomy operations, he can tell his patient with a great deal of accuracy whether his particular operation will be successful. A good lawyer should be able to advise his clients, with a high degree of accuracy, their chances of winning a suit.

In all of these examples, the person involved is dealing in most cases with highly *predictable* variables. Bringing their knowledge into the stock market usually results in the following effect: the first we noted above in the case of the engineer who made thousands of calculations in order to be successful in building a bridge but entered a stock purchase on no more than a chance reading of a favorable article in the local paper. He assumes that stock movements are based on a set of highly predictable facts. Quite the contrary is true. Stock price movement is based on many extremely *non-predictable* variables, the most important one being what people *think*—which in some cases has no relation whatsoever to the particular company itself.

A great part of our problem then becomes a study of what affects people and how they typically react. To better illustrate, here is a baffling phenomenon to the beginning investor: notice what happened to the price of stocks in general the day President Kennedy was assassinated. Within moments of the first news release, prices plunged drastically, resulting in an immediate decision by the Board of Governors to close the New York Stock Exchange 17 minutes later. Yet in those brief few minutes, the Dow Jones Industrial Average dropped 21.16 points or 2.89%, and 2,200,000 shares were traded. Delta Airlines dropped 11¼ points (almost 20%), RCA dropped 5½ points (6%), Polaroid 16 points (10%), and U.S. Steel 4⅜ points (10%).

The question here is why would people sell in panic after such news. Certainly the value of the companies had not changed in those few minutes, and yet it was later reported by Exchange personnel that the majority of their orders were "sell" and "cancel buy."

To understand stock market logic then, the *first step* is to realize that the most important variable is what people think. The second step is to analyze what variables affect people's thinking, the most important of which are the emotions of fear and greed. The emotion that took hold in the Kennedy assassination was fear—and the average investor's reaction to fear is to raise *cash* by selling. It may be argued that this doesn't make much sense. However, in the development of stock market logic it must be clearly understood that the emotion of fear forces the average investor to sell.

Don't bet against falling prices as the first and most immediate reaction to fear situations, e.g., a Presidential heart attack, wars, natural disasters, etc. The Kennedy assassination is a classic in this regard, and differs from all other shocks of a 30-year period in that it was completely unpredictable and not anticipated. It required the closing of the New York Stock Exchange for the first time since 1933 due to heavy volume selling. This was not the case with Pearl Harbor, Roosevelt's death, Korea, Cuba or even the more recent escalation in Viet Nam, though in fact most of these events had far greater economic consequences in regard to stock prices than did the loss of a youthful president. The difference is that in each of these cases, the astute investor had sufficient advance information to bring to his calculations the possibility of entering war, or the death of a President who had been ailing for many months. Still, the first and immediate reaction to the *fact* that we were going into war was again a drop in stock prices. The drop was softened by the fact that the cool and calculated buyers, who had been selling at the first "hint" of war or trouble ahead, were taking advantage of the fear emotion by buying at reduced prices.

Thus we have the phenomenon of sluggish or slightly declining prices as news of *possible* involvement in Viet Nam began to leak out of various official sources in the spring of 1965. Prices began to fall more sharply as the news worsened. Then suddenly the President announced it was official; now the war in Viet Nam is going to worsen and we are going to send in more troops. The facts are out; there is no more guessing or uncertainty. Stock prices go up. This is stock market logic in action and don't bet against it. This type of action and reaction has fostered several proverbs: "buy rumor, sell news," "buy strike news, sell settlement," "buy bad news, sell good news," etc.

I hasten to add that there certainly are exceptions to the above oversimplification, but I might recommend that you don't bet against these adages; their batting average is about 75% correct.

It is this same concept that baffles the beginner when he reads a glowing report about a company's sales, earnings, or new contracts, only to watch the price go down. Or in reverse, he reads a less glowing report, only to watch the price move up. It may appear on the surface to be an illogical situation, but is in fact quite the contrary. Stock prices move in anticipation of good news and if the tyro would take a moment to investigate he is likely to find that the stock that looked so good in print has in fact been moving up rapidly, possibly for weeks or months. Then ask this question: What more good news might be anticipated in the immediate future to keep this stock moving up? Who is likely to sell to me on such good news? If this doesn't sober your enthusiasm in search for the answers, then I suggest that you hold your breath and wait three days: the odds are you will buy it lower within three to five days. Try it sometime.

Obviously, there are always exceptions—where good news is really good news—but again in most cases it happens where predictability is slim. This often occurs, e.g., in the case of new mineral or oil discoveries.

In the case of bad news, the beginner should ask himself: "What worse news is likely to drive the price of a stock lower in the immediate future?" If he can't think of any, then maybe the worst is over; the bottom may have been reached.

The stock market remains, then, a most logical place to do business. The trick is to know and to be able to apply "stock market logic" as opposed to general business logic. It should only make sense that the man who makes money by building bridges does so in keen competition with others in a similar field. But when that same person steps into another field of endeavor, he is also in a competitive situation where other men, more skilled than he, will in the long run end up with all the profits, which prompts another adage of proven value: "If it is so easy to make money in the stock market, how come everybody ain't rich?"

It *ain't* easy!

Chapter II

GENERAL MARKET PERSPECTIVE

Now that we have briefly reviewed the stock market "facts of life," so to speak, it is important that we become more specific and gain a general market perspective. On Page 13 there is a 36-year panorama of various investment markets, represented by the Dow Jones Industrial, Transportation and Utility Averages, along with the British Industrial Average and a low-priced stock index. This very graphic chart is on a semi-logarithmic scale which means that the percentage change of various moves becomes directly comparable, regardless of different price scales. Several minutes' careful study of this picture should be made beginning with the Dow Jones Industrial Average at the top of the page.

Note first the long-long trend has been generally higher. The bottom in 1942 was at a level of approximately 95 (scale at far left or right hand columns; date by month at the bottom) and the recent top of 1973 was about 1,050. Thus we conclude that the *average* of stocks that comprise this Average has risen approximately 1,000% during this period. Be careful of such calculations and do not assume that every stock has made this rise, as again this is an average of the high quality companies listed on p. 14.

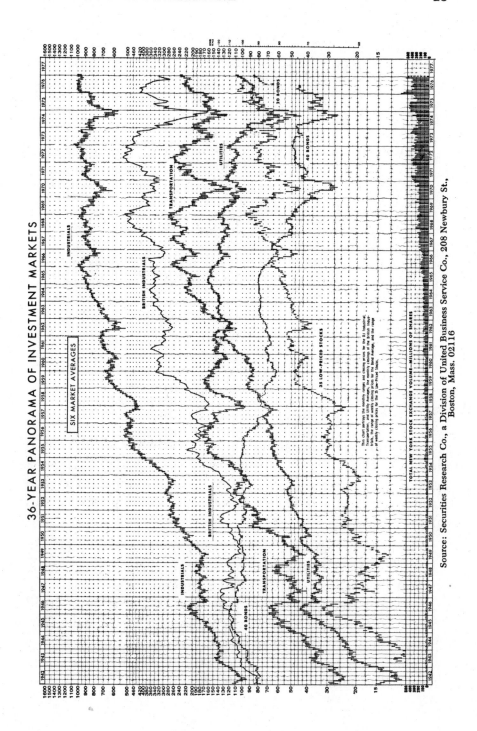

36-YEAR PANORAMA OF INVESTMENT MARKETS

SIX MARKET AVERAGES

Source: Securities Research Co., a Division of United Business Service Co., 208 Newbury St., Boston, Mass. 02116

List of Dow Jones Industrial Average
Stocks as of February, 1977
(Divisor: 1.504)

Allied Chemical   Inco
Aluminum Co.   International Harvester
American Can   International Paper
American Tel. & Tel.   Johns-Manville
American Brands   Minnesota Mining
Bethlehem Steel   Owens-Illinois
Chrysler Corp.   Proctor & Gamble
Du Pont   Sears, Roebuck
Eastman Kodak   Standard Oil of Calif.
Esmark   Texaco
Exxon   Union Carbide
General Electric   United Technologies
General Foods   U. S. Steel
General Motors   Westinghouse Electric
Goodyear   Woolworth

Several have done far in excess of 1000% and a few somewhat less. But broadly speaking, the past 36 year period has been a good period for rising common stock prices, and that is the main conclusion that should be drawn from a first glance at this panorama.

I can hear some grumbles already that the Dow Jones Industrial Average is a poor representative of the average stock, or that the Standard & Poor's 500 is superior, or that it is out of date—and I could not agree more. But in developing a broad perspective about general swings of the past, I believe the Dow Jones Industrial Average does a very adequate job.

Our next step is to mark the bottoms of the various downswings that occurred during this 36 year period. Also make a note of the month in which they occurred. We find that in the past 36 years the general market has been at a major bottom (thus the ideal time for aggressive buying) eleven times, or approximately three times in a 10-year span. The market for the previous 60 years suggests this concept has a high degree of reliability. This becomes rather important. Assuming the average investor doesn't begin to accumulate much in the way of investment funds until the age of 35 or later, and assuming that the ideal time for buying follows the pattern of only three major buying opportunities per decade, think what this means to you during *your* investment lifetime. Assume you begin your investing career at the age of 35 and that you live three score and ten years. Then during your investment lifetime you should have only *ten* ideal general market buying opportunities. Now think at your current age how many such opportunities you may have left.

This concept is important from several points of view. First, these major bottoms do not occur very often, and secondly, you must be able to recognize them in their early stages in order to take the utmost advantage of them. These buying opportunities always occur as the aftermath of a down phase, during which you may have in fact lost money, and just when things seem the blackest, actually the probabilities are now swinging heavily in your favor. I suggest that you commit these bottom periods, both years and months, to memory so that in our study ahead when working with individual stocks you can draw some rapid conclusions concerning the individual stock movement as compared to the general market.

The next step in grasping the over-all perspective of the market is to pick out the approximate topping zones during this 36 year period. Note the year and month that the tops occurred. At once it becomes obvious that tops are harder to locate precisely than bottoms. But during your study you have witnessed approximately seven significant topping periods. The thing is to determine how long the rising phases are, meaning bottom to top, and then how long from the top back down to the bottom again.

Rising Periods (bottom to top)	Percentage Increase	Approx. No. of YEARS
April, 1942 - June, 1946	110%	4
June, 1949 - Jan., 1953	90%	3½
Sept., 1953 - April, 1956	110%	2½
Oct., 1957 - Aug., 1959	60%	2
Oct., 1960 - Nov. 1961	30%	1
May, 1962 - Jan., 1966	90%	3½
Oct., 1966 - Dec., 1968	30	2
May, 1970 - Jan., 1973	65	2½
Dec., 1974 - ?		

Declining Periods (top to bottom)	Percentage Decrease	Approx. No. of MONTHS
July, 1946 - Oct., 1946*	25%	4
Jan., 1953 - Sept., 1953	20%	8
July, 1957 - Oct., 1957**	20%	3
Jan., 1960 - Oct., 1960	18%	8
Nov., 1961 - May, 1962	30%	7
Jan., 1966 - Oct., 1966	25%	8
Dec., 1968 - May, 1970	35	17
Jan., 1973 - Dec., 1974	45	23

*The period that followed the bottom in 1946 is termed a sideways trading range, meaning little upside or downside progress, for approximately three years.
**The period April, 1956, to June, 1957, is again a sideways trading market lasting approximately one year.

Several fairly valid conclusions can be drawn from this approach. First, stocks are generally in a rising phase approximately 75% of the time and the longest rising span of the past 36 years was approximately four years in duration. The shortest was approximately one year with the average rising period lasting a little over two and a half years.

This logically leads us to define more clearly the words "long term" as they will be applicable for the remainder of this book. In most any discussion with a group of investors, someone will undoubtedly say he is a "long term investor." This concept has wide and varied meaning to different individuals; some use the phrase to mean five to ten years or longer, some mean a one-year period as established by the capital gains tax laws, and still others will mean one to three years.

Throughout this book I shall use the phrase *long-long term* to denote a period generally five years or longer.

Long term is a period of time not less than one year nor more than four with an average of approximately two and a half. This typically tends to coincide with the rising phases of the general market during the past two and a half decades.

Intermediate term: 60-120 days.

Any shorter duration will be referred to as day-to-day or *short term*.

The second significant conclusion we can draw from the panorama chart is that while the general movement is declining only 25% of the time or less, it occurs very swiftly, lasting only three to twenty three months or an average of ten months. This is significant in bringing some credence to such old stock market sayings as: "Buy late, sell early," "If there is any doubt, get out," "Don't overstay the market," "Stocks come down three times faster than they go up."

Some additional conclusions can be drawn from this panorama of mass market movements by study of the interrelationships between the Industrial, Transportation and Utility Averages. Looking at all the Averages together, we can conclude that they all tend to move in the same direction at approximately the same time. The magnitude of the swings is noticeably different. The Utility Average is extremely stable, at least in comparison to the widely swinging Transportation Average. The Industrials appear to be somewhat of a compromise in volatility between the Transportation and Utility Averages.

The next conclusion that can be drawn from this study is that stocks, regardless of basic industries, move in the same direction at the same time and they tend to reach their major bottoms and tops approximately together. They are more likely to hit bottoms together than tops.

A comparison of the listed markets' movements, as represented by the Dow Jones Industrial Average, with the Over-the-Counter Market, as represented by the National Quotation Bureau Index of Over-the-Counter stocks, leads to the conclusion that the Over-the-Counter stocks also tend to move in the same direction as listed markets at the same time.

The above concepts should not in any way be construed to imply that all stocks or industry groups will be rising at the same time, but that the majority will be moving higher during the same period. In most cases the batting average will be between 65 to 85%. This obviously leaves plenty of room for 15 to 35% of stock issues to be moving sideways or lower. More important, however, if 65 to 85% of the stocks are moving higher, then your odds of picking a winner are certainly greatly enhanced.

Look at a down phase. It will be a lot tougher to make profits if 65% of the issues are in fact declining, but it can be done because there have always been a few groups that will rise when the others are falling.

The major point in our discussion of a general market perspective, however, is to attempt to have as many positive factors as possible on our side before we make an investment commitment, and certainly some discussion and knowledge of the pattern of mass stock movements is essential. Our task is to become fully and aggressively invested in the first few months following a major market bottom, and to become conservative or defensive at market tops.

Chapter III

LONG TERM INDICATORS

It shall be the goal of the several investment blueprints discussed in later chapters to coincide the majority of long term investment buying to the general market bottoms as closely as possible. You will find also that several of the different types of securities are historically at their bottoms at the same time the mass movement of stocks bottoms out. For these reasons, then, I shall put forth some stock market indicators that have a good batting average for telling you when you are at or near the bottom of the general downswing. Now I did not say that these indicators would send up a flare or shoot off a cannon at the precise bottom. I said they have a good record of suggesting the approach of a general market low point. I do not suggest that you are likely to, or should even attempt to, make all your purchases right on the bottom. Actually, as we will see in our study of group movement, it usually takes several weeks or months past the bottom to discover which groups are likely to lead the way in the new bull market. However, like it or not, the mass movement of stocks has an inescapable influence on most all stocks, even if only for extremely short periods of time.

But, more importantly, the general market typically has a far greater psychological impact on *you* as an investor than the specific movement of the stocks in your portfolio. Time and time again people have come to me and said, "The *market* looks high," or more typically at the bottom of the downswing,

"This *market* looks like it is going straight down; I think I should sell all my stocks."

I'm sure if you have been investing for some years that some of you may be guilty of selling out near the bottom and in most cases a great deal of the emotional pressure that brought you to this decision was not so much the fact that your particular stocks were down, but that many stocks were falling and you wanted either to "get out before your stocks crashed," or to "salvage something" on the thought that something now is better than nothing later. These are emotional responses, particularly when the evening news tells you that for several weeks, with only minor upswings, "the market" — meaning the Dow Jones Industrial Average — "was down again today in active trading."

If you can learn from the start to recognize that few persons can escape this emotional fear selling, then you become better equipped to cope with it and possibly to turn it to your advantage. Today, as an example, when the pressure to sell is the greatest, that is when I start shaking my head and begin to state, "It should hold here." When I rush to the brokerage office a half hour before opening time to be sure I am there to watch the crash, when I feel my stomach turn and food doesn't appeal to me, when the blood is rushing to my head and my breathing is a little short because I know I must make a decision, possibly to "salvage what is left," when my broker's voice is trembling, when the faces in the board room are full of fear: then, I have *learned* this is not the time to sell. THIS IS THE TIME TO BUY.

This is an educated calculation that has proven correct with an almost perfect batting average. Yet it is difficult to ignore the emotions involved in watching your holdings while other stocks are dropping rather sharply in price and in unison. The important thing is that *learning* to recognize and control your emotions *will make you money* and, after all, that is why you are reading this book.

It is true that where our money is concerned we do become emotional, and this is why we turn to a discussion of indicators. Stock market indicators are no more or less than the interaction of certain data that have had a history of repeating their performances over many stock market swings. These indicators can be helpful in controlling emotions and in more precisely pinpointing the bottoms and tops. They can be divided basically into long and intermediate term indicators.

The indicators that will be discussed were selected for their high degree of accuracy and because of the ready availability of the data needed to compute them. Most of this data may be obtained from a local paper or the Wall Street Journal. This leaves a few indicators which have not been elaborated upon because the average investor is unlikely to have the time or availability of information to make the necessary computations. The indicators which will be discussed should give you some good weapons with which to wage the battle for investment survival.

Bad News, but Rising
Prices Indicator

Keep in mind that our basic goal is to buy low, not necessarily on the bottom, but more specifically in the first few months of the new upswing. Keep in mind also that a general downswing has typically reached bottom with no *specific reasons* or news items to account for the down move. Now, already at or near the bottom, the bad news begins to appear. At this point the market is moving sideways or slightly higher as the new upswing gets underway. The question you must ask yourself is why are stocks not moving down but instead moving up. The *fact* that stocks are gradually and steadily moving higher in the face of bad economic or political news is one of the best indicators that you have passed the bottom and are, in fact, probably in the early stages of a new upswing. This is known as the *Bad News, but Rising Prices Indicator*, and it is quite reliable on a long term basis. As the average long term major upswing will last approximately two and a half years, becoming aggressively invested even in the first six months is your basic objective.

This indicator is primarily a psychological one and there is, therefore, no specific way of measuring it.

New Lows Indicator

Another indicator that typically pinpoints major bottoms (but you won't be sure of it for several weeks) is the *New Lows Indicator*. Each day in most major metropolitan papers and of course in the Wall Street Journal you can find a section that will tell you how many stocks on the New York Stock Exchange made new high prices or new low prices for the year. General market bottoms are occurring when many stocks are making new lows. Observation of the past market bottoms leads to the conclusion that when the daily new lows begin to exceed 300 per day, a market bottom may be close at hand. Should the figure of new daily lows be in excess of 300, e.g., 350, 500, 1,000 or more, for several days during a four week period, then wake up—because the bottom is at hand or close by.

Looking back you will probably find that the actual bottom for the Dow Jones Industrial Average and the maximum day for new lows occurred together. With a few battle scars to remind me, I strongly recommend that you make no attempt to second guess when the maximum number of new lows has or will occur. I remember only too well in May of 1962 when, by tradition, the new low indicator was suggesting a bottom—then the sky fell in. It was the bottom all right, but if you had jumped in a bit early you could have taken a pretty good bath in the few days that followed. By the middle of June the storm had passed and most prices were still close to their lows established in May. This was the time for calculated, non-emotional buying. Follow the old adage: "Buy late, sell early."

The New Lows Indicator is a good indicator. Use it wisely, slowly, and in conjunction with others. One word of caution about its use. Remember that in order to arrive at a major market bottom, the averages will usually have to have been dropping for several months. When they reach the point where the new lows are in excess of the magnitude indicated, for about two to four weeks, then the conclusion applies. Should an intermediate sell-off occur that produces in excess of 200 to 300 new lows on a one-day basis, but does not repeat within the next several weeks, the probabilities are you have ridden through an intermediate dip that has none of the *long term* implications. This indicator can be useful for the intermediate term, but I feel it is better for long term considerations.

New Highs vs. New Lows

An excellent indicator that may be used to confirm that a major bottom has been passed is the number of new highs in relation to new lows. In order to be in a solid rising market it is necessary for more stocks to be advancing than declining, and thus new highs must exceed new lows by a considerable margin. Within a matter of only *two* to *four* weeks past the bottom, the following should confirm the uptrend: first, new lows contract sharply from 300 to 1,000 per day down to 20 to 40 per day. At the same time, new highs will expand from 0 to 10-15 per day. Secondly, new lows and new highs become approximately equal with about 20 new highs and 20 new lows. Next, and surprisingly typical, only three to four weeks past the actual day of the bottom, new highs begin to outnumber new lows by a wide margin. Now this plurality of new highs over new lows must continue to expand during the months ahead.

The maximum number of new highs occurs approximately half the distance from the bottom to the top in the averages. Thus, new highs are helpful in determining the mid-point in the rise, not the top.

Volume

Turn back to the 36 year panorama on Page 13 and at the bottom of the chart you will see vertical lines which represent the monthly total volume traded on the New York Stock Exchange. The volume is reported daily, again in most local financial sections and in the Wall Street Journal. Volume is a relative matter. As you will rapidly note, volume has been steadily rising for the entire period shown. This should be no surprise; after all, we have many more stocks listed on the New York Stock Exchange than we did 36 years ago and we have many times more people wanting to invest. As a matter of fact, the reason this has been a general long-long term period of rising stock prices is because there just hasn't been a sufficient supply of stocks available to satisfy the people who want to own them on a long-long term basis.

Take a straight edge and draw a line from a general market bottom in the Averages down to the volume. Now, in relation to the volume that preceded and followed each market bottom, was the volume at the bottom relatively high or low? The answer is low. Thus, the conclusion is that at major market bottoms, the volume will be relatively low. Next note what the volume was doing in the early stage of the new upswing. Was it expanding or contracting? The answer is expanding. This leads to the conclusion that *one prime ingredient of a new bull market is expanding volume.* This volume indicator is one of the *most* reliable you can count on.

Finally, study where the volume reaches its maximum. If your conclusion is on the top, you are wrong. Typically, volume reaches its maximum intensity at a point which appears to be approximately half way the distance from the bottom to the top of each long term swing. How can this fact be helpful? As long as volume continues to expand we have not reached this half way point in the upward cycle. Or, when volume begins to contract for several months (three to five), the probabilities favor the fact that the half way point in the market upswing was reached during the month or months of peak volume.

This concept of a half way point in the total market upswing thus becomes helpful in establishing approximately the topping area; e.g., the low in the Dow Jones Industrial Average in 1958 was approximately 420. The peak midpoint volume occurred in approximately the 550 area, or 130 points above the low. The estimated top area should be approximately 130 points above the midpoint prices, or 680. In the 1958-1960 upswing this measurement worked out almost perfectly. These estimates will not usually have such a perfect batting average as in the example above, but they warn of a coming top.

During a decline in the general market, volume typically contracts except during emotional or panic selling waves, which seldom last more than a few days. Be careful not to attempt to apply general market volume considerations to individual stocks. They are *not* the same. How do you get this monthly volume figure? If you don't have a broker or service that provides the information, then add it up daily.

Short Interest Ratio

When discussing the Short Interest Ratio Indicator, it is assumed that persons reading this book understand what "short sale" means and how mechanically it is accomplished. The short

interest is no more than the composite total of all issues on the
New York Stock Exchange having 5,000 or more of their shares
sold short and reported by various brokerage firms to the Exchange the 15th of each month. Understand that these reports
count the outstanding short sales as of the close on the 15th of
each month, not how many may have occurred during the
reporting period.

As there is no time limit on a short sale (assuming stock can
be borrowed), some of the shorts reported may be months or
even years outstanding and others only a day or so old. In any
case, each broker must report the total number of shares in
every stock where his clients have made short sales. These are
totaled by the New York Stock Exchange and all those that have
a "short position" of 5,000 shares or more are reported as the
"short interest" about the 18th of each month. The "short interest" is the total of these outstanding short sales, and if divided
by the average daily New York Stock Exchange volume for the
preceding month, will give you the *Short Interest Ratio.*

The Short Interest Ratio has been used more successfully
as an indicator than just the short interest itself, because the
ratio adjusts for the different volumes of stocks being considered. This is important because 30 years ago the average daily
volume was only 500,000 to 1,000,000 shares, whereas today it
is averaging over twenty million.

To truly understand the value of this indicator, it must be
understood that the general market is usually at the bottom
when the news is the blackest and the mass of people "feel" it
will continue to go lower. At this precise moment, we typically
have the majority of emotional investors doing the wrong thing
and selling short, when in fact they should be buying. Emotional feelings cannot compete with cold, hard logic on a long
term basis.

The Short Interest Ratio has for many years tended to
swing between a high ratio of 2.0 and a low of 1.0. The reading

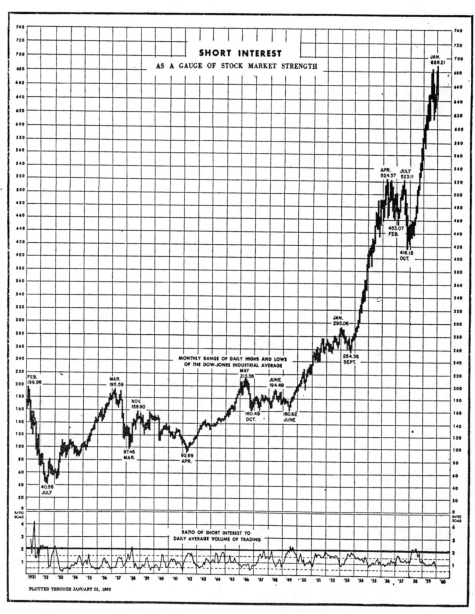

Source: Francis I. duPont & Co., One Wall St., New York, N. Y.

of 2.0 typically occurs at or close to major bottoms. As this data is reported only once each month, its interpretation is primarily for long term consideration.

Several possible conclusions may be drawn about the Short Interest Ratio. First, a relatively high Short Interest Ratio exists when the ratio is 1.70 or above. A reading of approximately 2.0 has been its upper limit going all the way back to 1931, when an exception to this concept existed as the Short Interest Ratio climbed to a 4.0 reading near the bottom of the 1929 collapse, which occurred in 1931.

Secondly, a major bottom has not been reached until the Short Interest Ratio is 1.70 or above.

Thirdly, the larger the Short Interest Ratio at the bottom, the longer and higher the bull market that follows is likely to be. The Short Interest Ratio will not pinpoint a bottom as closely as the New Lows Indicator. It has an excellent record of giving a definite clue to major bottoms, and our objective is not to hit the bottom precisely but to recognize the proximity of one and become aggressively invested as soon as possible.

The Short Interest Ratio also has a good record of indicating a warning near the tops. This is not nearly as precise as it is on the bottoms, but good enough for consideration, and used with other indicators, it should lead to a general conclusion of when to be a bit cautious. A reading of 1.0 or less appears to be the figure to keep in mind. A reading of .5 is double warning of an impending top. The record of this indicator is too good to ignore. You may not get out on the absolute top nor back in on the precise bottom, but in either case don't fight a record such as the Short Interest Ratio has attained or you are likely to be mowed down as the trend rolls over you.

The whole concept of the Short Interest Ratio is that mass opinion is usually wrong and the Short Interest Ratio is a practical measurement of bearish and bullish sentiment. If this still doesn't make sense to you logical beginners, who have yet to experience the emotions of a bottom, and are shaking your heads on how stupid one would be to sell short after the market has already dropped considerably and is in fact on the bottom, remember there is no one to tell you it is the bottom. The majority of investors will never read this book or any other that might give them a clue. But the fact remains, as the graph clearly indicates, that many people are betting the market will go lower right at the bottom.

There is another factor to consider in this concept. A lot of short sales means in effect potential future buyers, as they buy to cover their short positions. Thus should the market turn up, the shorts will typically buy back in to avoid further loss, or if it goes lower, they become tempted to take profits; thus at some point they become buyers. Again, back to basics, if you have buyers in excess of sellers, prices go up.

As I am attempting to present indicators that have outstanding batting averages and that are readily available, this is one of the best. All you have to know are the various limits and the interpretation. Ask your broker once a month to get you the Short Interest Ratio and apply the conclusions about levels discussed above. A word of caution: traditional levels can be broken. There may come a time again when the Short Interest Ratio will approach the 4.0 level. To do this will in all probability require a general market break of significant magnitude, not necessarily equal to the 1929 debacle, but certainly greater than those we have seen since. The important thing is that the level of the indicator is likely to be at its highest point close to the bottom. Following the axiom of "buy late, sell early" will allow a short time period to see if the indicator has clearly reached its zenith before committing one's entire fortune. The most common human reaction at the bottom is to search for

reasons to explain the previous drop. As the bad news begins to
tell you why, the next reaction is one of total disbelief as prices
begin to move higher.

Advance-Decline Indicator

The Advance-Decline Indicator is constructed by taking
each day the difference between those stocks which advanced
for the day and those which declined. This information is generally found in most major city papers on the financial page and
on the inside of the last page of the Wall Street Journal. These
differential figures are totaled each day and, if plotted on a
graph, will comprise a chart line such as the one on Page 31.
Looking at the advances vs. the declines each day or week is
the best way to establish whether the mass movement of stocks
is generally up or down or sideways. By looking at the total
number of stocks advancing, you can establish the approximate
probabilities as to whether your stocks are moving with or
against the mass trend.

As an example, if—of 1,300 issues traded—650 advanced and
650 declined, your batting average for that day or week or
month was probably no better than 50%. If the figure was 900
advances and 400 declines, then the odds are heavily on your
side of having made a profit for the time period considered.

On P.31. is a statistical table of information taken from the
Wall Street Journal. This table provides the information neces-
sary to compute the Advance-Decline Line and the daily New
Highs vs. New Lows, plus other data.

The Advance-Decline Indicator is a far better method of determining what the direction of the mass stock trend is than the
popular averages. For example, if you have ten stocks all selling
for ten dollars per share, on one day the average is $10. Assume
that the next day, nine of the issues go down one point and one
of the issues goes up ten points to $20. The average for the day

MARKET DIARY

	..Wed.	Tue.	Mon.	Fri.	Thu.	Wed.
Issues traded	1,849	1,857	1,878	1,849	1,843	1,885
Advances	651	485	442	972	601	375
Declines	691	888	994	438	759	1,051
Unchanged	507	484	442	439	483	459
New highs, 1977	23	17	31	34	20	27
New lows, 1977	114	181	121	69	151	129

DOW JONES CLOSING AVERAGES

		– – –WEDNESDAY– – –		
		1977	–Change–	1976
Industrials	....	914.73 – 1.41	–0.15%	986.22
Transportation	....	222.78 – 0.39	–0.17%	207.97
Utilities	....	107.14 + 0.16	+0.15%	86.98
Composite	....	302.89 – 0.32	–0.11%	301.28

OTHER MARKET INDICATORS

			1977	–Change–	1976
N.Y.S.E.	Composite	....	53.26 – 0.04	–0.08%	54.50
	Industrial	....	57.77 – 0.06	–0.10%	60.84
	Utility	....	39.92 – 0.01	–0.03%	35.72
	Transportation		40.03 + 0.05	+0.13%	38.84
	Financial	....	53.35 – 0.03	–0.06%	53.67
Amer. Ex. Mkt Val Index			110.81 – 0.08	–0.07%	103.97
Nasdaq OTC Composite		..	93.89 + 0.23	+0.25%	90.80
	Industrial	....	96.73 + 0.32	+0.33%	97.92
	Insurance	....	96.79 + 0.62	+0.64%	91.01
	Banks	....	89.70 – 0.14	–0.16%	83.28
Stand. &	Poor's 500	......	97.91 – 0.10	–0.10%	102.21
	400 Industrial	..	108.72 – 0.15	–0.14%	114.99

TRADING ACTIVITY

Volume of advancing stocks on N.Y.S.E., 6,210,000 shares; volume of declining stocks, 7,560,000. On American S.E., volume of advancing stocks, 850,000; volume of declining stocks, 750,000. Nasdaq volume of advancing stocks, 2,602,600; volume of declining stocks, 1,177,000.

would be 10.2; but unless you held the one big winner, it was in fact a day where your chances of making a profit were only 10%.

A study of the major market Averages vs. the Advance-Decline Line is presented on Page 32. Note that the Average and the Advance-Decline Line typically hit bottom at approximately the same time. But also note carefully that the Advance-Decline Line begins to level off and move sideways several

MAJOR MARKET AVERAGES
AND STOCK MARKET BREADTH

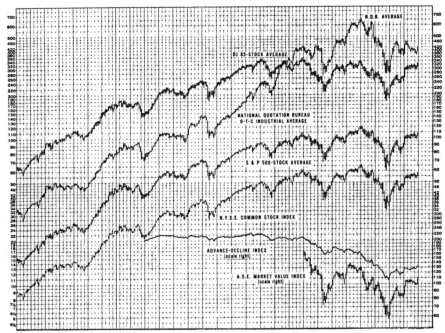

Source: Securities Research Co., a Division of United Business Service Co., 208 Newbury St., Boston, Mass. 02116

months or even a year or so in advance of the Average top. This phenomenon implies that in the early stages of a new bull market the odds are heavily in favor of your making money.

These odds may reach 80% or better during the early phase of the rise, but then begin to slip back slowly, even as the Average continues higher. By the time you reach the top in the Average, the odds have shifted slowly from 80% in your favor to approximately 60% or more against you. It may be wondered how the Average can continue to rise as the top is approached when in fact the majority of stocks may be declining. This occurs as follows: assume that steels and oils within the Average are the early leaders that are advancing sharply from the bottom. The papers and autos have stopped going down and begin to move sideways. The Average rises because of the early strong leadership of oils and steels. Then assume that these early leaders begin to tire and move sideways, just as the papers and auto stocks turn strong. The steels and oils will no longer be advancing but as yet have not begun to fall. Thus the papers and autos carry the Average into new high ground.

From the absolute bottom to a mythical point approximately half way between the bottom and the top in the Average, the majority of stocks are advancing, reaching a maximum probability factor of approximately 80% (seldom above 80% as even in a bull market about 10 to 20% of the issues will be neutral or declining.)

This simply means that while it is more difficult to lose money in a bull market, the selection of individual groups and issues is still the most important consideration. If this is so, you may be wondering why we are spending so much time on general market factors and not spending all of our time studying groups and individual stocks. The answer, like it or not, is simply because the mass movement has its effect on all stocks even though it may be only to slow the upward progress or accelerate the downside drop. But what is more important is the psychological effect the general movement has on you as a prospective buyer or seller. Let's face it; we don't operate in a vacuum and the general movement is affected by many factors that do not necessarily pertain to the success of any individual company.

If an investor owned a ten-stock portfolio during a sharply falling general market and seven of his stocks were declining, two were standing still, and one was moving higher, what do you think his reaction to such a situation would be? Without reservation, I say the average investor will sell first the one that is moving slowly higher, on the rationalization that he had better sell that one before it begins to drop or while he "can still take a profit."

Next, the two that are standing still will be sold for similar reasons. And, finally, the seven that are dropping sharply will be held "until they rally back" or "until I can get out even," or some such rationalization. As we will learn later in our study of trends, this is absolutely the wrong approach. Anyone who says that mass movement of stocks is unimportant (while in ivory tower theory it is possibly correct) doesn't truly understand that stocks are bought and sold by people who observe and whose judgment is affected by what other stocks or people are doing.

The Advance-Decline Line is one of the best guides to determine if the odds are in your favor, on balance, or running against you. As long as the Advance-Decline Line continues to make new highs every two or three months, the tide is running strongly in your favor. However, after the Advance-Decline Line fails to make a significant new high within a six-month period, the caution flag is raised and much more attention must be given to selectivity and appraisal of downside risk. Generally, there will not be any great cause for alarm at this point as not much downside pressure is likely to occur. But there should be no doubt that it becomes increasingly more difficult to make money.

If the Dow Jones Industrial Average continues moving higher but the Advance-Decline Line continues sideways, then definite defensive steps should be taken to protect profits and shift to stocks with higher stability factors, high yielding bonds, or cash.

The considerations and conclusions above apply to long term major swings. Later a variation of this Advance-Decline Line will be discussed as an intermediate term indicator.

Economic Indicators

The indicators discussed above must be termed "stock market indicators," as distinguished from "economic indicators," which will be discussed very briefly below.

The stock market and the general economy are often inter-
mixed and considered to be the same thing. Nothing could be
further from the truth, yet each year and during each cycle
some supposedly very smart people make the mistake of not dis-
tinguishing between the two, and come home with far fewer
profits than they would have realized if they had done some
research.

Gross National Product

In recent years one of the most popular indicators measuring the strength or weakness of the *economy* is the Gross National Product (GNP). This expresses the sum total of all goods
and services produced in the United States.

Below is a graph of the GNP covering approximately 12
years. The shaded zones indicate periods of time which the
Bureau of Economic Research calls recession or depression
phases. Now, it is very important to compare the movements of
the GNP with those of the general market. The heavy vertical
lines mark the bottom in the stock market downswing. Note
that almost without exception the market was at the bottom of
its swing when the GNP was just *beginning* to level out or drop.

GROSS NATIONAL PRODUCT

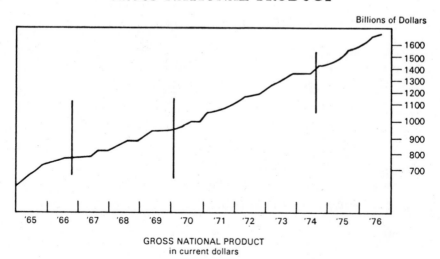

GROSS NATIONAL PRODUCT
in current dollars

Remember for the market to be at the bottom, it must have been falling for several months, or while the GNP was still moving higher.

You can imagine the confusion when the economists are telling you that everything is rosy, but each morning when you call your broker, he tells you that your stocks are dropping lower. What do you do? Whom do you believe? This can't happen, you think. But it does—about three times every ten years, just far enough apart for you to forget how it was the last time. The next thing that happens is that the economists begin to see the errors in their calculations and, as no one likes to be wrong, the errors are typically blamed on some unforeseen event that changed the course of the economy to sideways or down.

About this time the market is already at or close to its bottom. Big money, not knowing for sure but anticipating the possibility of an economic downturn, had sold out earlier and is now ready to buy back in at reduced prices. The general economic news worsens and the mass of people become aware that the GNP is dropping. Now, big money is again back buying stocks at lower levels. Thus, in the face of a declining GNP, stocks begin to move sideways and then up, again in anticipation of better economic conditions.

Unemployment

Another economic indicator that in recent years has also been used to determine just how healthy the economy is, is the unemployed labor force. The lower the rate of *unemployment*, the healthier the economy and vice versa. While this may be true of the economy, note that at the very top of the stock market we have the fewest unemployed and that at the bottom the figure is still relatively low. Note also that during the first stage of the new bull market the unemployment figures are rising sharply. If you heard for several months that unemploy-

ment continued to worsen as the level of the economy dropped
into a recession phase, how tough it would be for you to view
these economic facts as good for stock price movement. So
look closely the *facts* are before you.

The conclusion we can draw from these comparisons is that
the stock market is the *barometer* or forecaster of the economy,
not the mirror. A count of business cycles back to 1900 indicates that the stock market turns up or down approximately
three to eight months ahead of the economy, with an average
of about five months. It is important that you clearly understand
this point in order to prepare yourself in advance not to be
snowed under by the waves of good economic news occurring
at or near the top, or the bad news that pours out during the
early stages of the next major rise.

There is nothing like experience when it comes to making
investment decisions in the stock market, but like any good
craftsman, the better you know how to use your tools, the more
successful you are likely to be. When several indicators are
suggesting that we are at or near a major bottom, then it is time
to stop, look, and listen. It is also time to act. I do not mean to
imply here a mad stampede to hock your house and your wife's
jewelry. If you feel confident that it *definitely* is the bottom,
look out! If you are not scared, it is probably not the bottom.

If along with that definitely "not sure" feeling, your tools
(indicators) say "now," then some action is demanded and that
action is to BUY. If the market and recent purchases continue
going down, then sell out at a 10-15% loss and wait for stronger
indicators. If, on the other hand, within several weeks you have
a profit and the market goes sideways or up in the face of very
bearish news, then buy some more, steadily and gradually committing yourself to a full bullish position as you gain profits.

In these few pages covering long term indicators, no attempt
has been made to cover all such possible indicators. As I assume

that the average reader of these pages will not be employing a full time computer or staff to cover all indicators, I have selected the ones that I have found to be most reliable and whose data is relatively easy to secure. As these indicators truly are most helpful only at major turns, they should only be referred to occasionally. They give one a general reference point concerning the major market movement.

Chapter IV

INTERMEDIATE INDICATORS

Before leaving the subject of stock market indicators, a discussion of two intermediate term indicators that are the best I have discovered should prove worthwhile. By definition, intermediate term is a period of approximately 60 to 120 days duration. I have found that a refinement of two of the long term indicators, using daily reported data, have proved excellent for determining these shorter term swings.

Remember, while major bottoms occur only three times in approximately ten years, intermediate term bottoms occur approximately two and a half times each year, or an average of five intermediate bottoms each two years. These indicators become much more important in our daily lives as they tend to help us to forecast the immediate time period ahead.

10-Day Advance-Decline Line

The first intermediate indicator is the 10-day Advance-Decline Line. This is constructed by simply running a differential of advances and declines for the previous ten day period. By no more than trial and error, I have discovered that this composite 10-day differential total tends to swing between a plus 3,000 (meaning that in the past ten days, 3,000 more stocks have advanced than declined) and minus 3,000 (meaning that during the past ten days, 3,000 more stocks have declined than advanced). This indicator has been a better buying indicator than a selling indicator. In practice, this is typically how it works. When we have reached the plus 3,000 area, stocks typically lose much of their steam and begin to go sideways or drop back slightly. No great downward pressure is usually witnessed; quite the contrary, most stocks are doing quite well. But their advance slows, drifts sideways, or actually falls back some.

At minus 3,000, however, the story has been quite different. When most stocks have sharply reacted to recent downside pressure in order to create this plurality of declines over advances, the general downswing is at its bottom and it is time for buying action. While no general intermediate sell signal is registered when this indicator stands at plus 3,000, it has been a typical intermediate buy signal when it registers in the approximately minus 3,000 area. This minus 3,000 phenomenon has usually occurred only two and a half times a year, thus giving us a gauge as to where we stand at any moment.

A "normal" swing of this indicator, starting at minus 3,000, would appear somewhat as follows. A sharp reversal of declines over advances is replaced by several days of advances over declines and this will break, in most cases, any descending trend that may be drawn from previous *over-bought* conditions of plus 3,000. It is *very important* to wait for a clear break of this trend to the upside. The reason is that minus 3,000 or that approximate area has a batting average that is about 70% correct, but on other occasions of extreme stress the magnitude may shift, as it did in May of 1962. Stepping into a minus 3,000 reading or better, without a clear change in the trend, was very unprofitable in early May, 1962. During the next few weeks the roof fell in, producing minus 6,000 declines over advances.

Be cautious of all arbitrary magnitudes as most will change their traditional levels or ratios during extreme stress periods. Thus it has proven to be more prudent to wait for a clear break to the upside of the 10-day Advance-Decline Line. Be alerted, however, that in the majority of intermediate bottoms it will start up from approximately the minus 2,500 to the minus 3,500 (oversold) level.

Once this trend is clearly broken — which should be about three to five days past the bottom — look back to the day of the absolute bottom as established by the 10-day Advance-Decline Line. Call this day Point "B" (for bottom) and start counting 60 to 120 calendar days forward. The minimum upswing from the oversold condition (minus 3,000) should last 60 days. A minimum intermediate upswing of only 60 days would be suggestive of long term weakness. The average intermediate upswing should last 90 to 120 calendar days from Point "B." An intermediate upswing not corrected (down dip) after 120 days would be indicative of long term power.

If one follows the axiom "buy late," and applies this also to the intermediate upswing, it should prove most profitable to allow Point "B" to clearly pass and then buy directly into the groups and individual stocks which display maximum strength at ten to 30 days past Point "B." This in my opinion is a much

more professional approach than to think that you missed the
whole shooting match by not buying on the exact day of the
bottom. Yet many people do just that.

Now, reaching 3,000 (overbought), the 10-day Advance-
Decline Line will typically pull back to approximately plus 500.
Then it will gradually rise again to approximately the plus 1,600
to 1,800 area, and then begin a slow downward drift pattern,
but still on the plus side for the next 60 to 120 days. Assuming
an average intermediate cycle of 100 days, the 10-day Advance-
Decline Line should be at approximately "0" (evenly balanced)
at 100 days past Point "B." At this point, no great down pressure
is usually evident, but most stocks are definitely moving sideways or slightly lower. About this time the 10-day Advance-
Decline Line will move again to the plus 500 area and this is
typically followed by another dip, this time to below the "0"
line. As the Advance-Decline Line dips below the "0" line at
this stage, usually the Dow Jones Industrial Average will also
begin to break downward out of a sideways movement. This
typically creates more selling and eventually results in another
intermediate bottom. Intermediate downswings generally last
30 to 60 days with an average of 45 days from top to bottom.
The above conclusions apply in a general rising, or bull market.
Intermediate upswings in a *bear market* typically last only 30
to 60 days.

Odd Lot Short Sales

Another intermediate indicator that works hand-in-glove
with the 10-day Advance-Decline Line is the Odd Lot Short
Sale Indicator. First determine what percent the daily odd lot
short sales are to the total odd lot sales (divide daily odd lot short
sales by total odd lot sales). Then construct a 10-day moving
average of the resultant figures. This indicator, like the Short
Interest Ratio, is a measurement of the prevailing bearish or bullish sentiment, but on a short or intermediate time basis. The
interpretation is also similar to the Short Interest Ratio as this
indicator typically swings between a reading of 2.0% at the bot-

tom of the intermediate downswing and .05% at the top of the swing. I have also called this indicator the "power indicator." As an example, after an intermediate decline of some proportions, *if* this indicator should read 4.0 to 6.0% (or higher) instead of 2.0%, this is an indication that the intermediate upswing is likely to be not only exceptionally strong, but is also apt to last longer than 120 days. As a matter of fact, major bull market bottoms will typically have an exceptionally high reading on this indicator.

The majority of the intermediate downswings, however, will typically show a reading on a 10-day basis of approximately 2.0%. When the 10-day Advance-Decline Line is registering a minus 2,000 and the 10-day Odd Lot Short Sales is at the 2.0% level, then the odds are about 85% that we are at or very close to an intermediate bottom.

As the upswing develops from Point "B" forward for approximately 100 days, this indicator gradually declines and has no particular significance during this period. When this indicator drops to a level near .05% and remains there for about two to four weeks, then another intermediate top is close at hand.

This indicator is much more precise in pinpointing the bottoms than the tops, but when used in close working relationship to the 10-day Advance-Decline Line, they comprise the best intermediate indicators I have yet found.

Summary of Long and
Intermediate Term Indicators

One final word regarding the use of indicators. They should be used as tools or guides to appraise the current intermediate and long term market situations. They should be appraised together and when the *majority* of indicators suggest a bottom or top approaching, then a plan of action, to be discussed in later chapters, should be put in motion. There are many indicators, as they have become quite popular in recent years. And again, I have discussed only those which I believe have excellent batting averages and where the information is easily accessible to you as a private investor. Should you find or have other indicators that you personally like and have found reliable, then by all means continue to use them and try those I have suggested above as back-up or confirmative indicators. In every major cycle that I have witnessed, at least one indicator has been out of gear with its traditional interpretation. Thus, having several tools instead of just one has much merit.

In developing or using new indicators, be sure to determine which point in the major swing it best identifies. If you will divide the major swings of the past into three major points, Point I indicating the bottoming area, Point II as a point approximately halfway between Points I and III, and Point III the topping area, I believe you will find that certain indicators will tend to pinpoint one of these major divisions more accurately than the other two. If you have never considered this concept of the midway point in a typical bull market, it can be most helpful in maintaining your overall perspective of the situation and, in most cases, will help to identify Point III.

The indicators which best suggest a midpoint in the market rise are:

1. Advance-Decline Line: peaks and begins to move sideways.
2. Monthly NYSE volume: peaks and begins to contract.
3. P/E Ratio of DJIA: peaks and begins to drop.
4. New Highs: maximum number occur.

This, then, is the story of indicators. Use them wisely, and with your psychological appraisal of the situation, they should provide you with excellent *tools* to sum up the market conditions as they develop. Don't become an "indicator nut," spending all your time and energy attempting to keep up or develop new ones, or you will go broke buying graph paper and pencils and will have completely defeated your prime objective and goal, which is to make money.

Chapter V

METHODS OF INDIVIDUAL STOCK SELECTION

Having gained a perspective of the general movement of the market and hopefully gained some tools by which to gauge this movement, it is now necessary to move on to the far more important task of determining which stocks you should buy.

Assume, for a moment, that the indicators were suggesting a bottoming area. The logical next step is, "What should I buy?" The majority of books that I have read about the stock market spend a great deal of time discussing "when" to buy individual issues. The authors have concluded that timing is the all-important factor in the quest for making money. Many have developed some very elaborate methods, using patterns, moving averages or volume. I call this a *timing* approach, and I will discuss it in a later chapter, but it typically does not help to answer the question "which stock to buy" or even point the investor in the right direction in order that he might be able to see the trees, not just the forest.

This book, then, hopes to fill the above void by devoting far greater time to the development of *selection* methods for individual stocks. This is particularly important to the long term, major cycle investor who is interested in holding an individual stock as long as the trend appears to be up. This usually means anywhere from a 50% to a 200% gain or more, thus leaving the 10% to 30% swings for so-called "traders."

The main methods for selection of stocks can be best broken down into three approaches:

1. Fundamental Approach.
2. Technical Approach.
3. Psychological Approach.

The Fundamental Approach deals with everything about the company itself. The Technical Approach deals strictly with the price and volume movement of the stock. And the Psychological Approach deals primarily with the emotional news factors that you as an investor must overcome.

Today we have individuals and firms devoting a great deal of time and energy to investment research. In many instances they typically favor one of the above approaches while ignoring or giving little weight to the other two. This, of course, is what makes the "horse race" and why you find one analyst telling you to buy a stock and another saying to sell the same issue. If you desire to discover how a particular investment man selects stocks, then ask him, "What method or yardstick do you use to select the stocks you buy or recommend?" If his answer primarily deals with the company, its products, earnings, management, dividends and various ratios, then his is a *Fundamental* approach. If his answer deals primarily with trends for the particular stock or industry group, or price patterns, then his approach is *Technical*. Should his answer be gauged by whether the news is either all bad or too rosy, then his is the *Psychological* approach, and he practices primarily the art of contrary opinion.

It is my belief that recognition of all three of these various approaches is important, and selection methods based on all three are likely to produce better results than just one. The next pages, therefore, will deal with what I consider to be the *best* features of each of these three approaches.

FUNDAMENTAL APPROACH

The fundamental or traditional approach is probably the most widely used today. We might even call it the textbook approach, as most all books written on the stock market until very recent years have stressed this approach in one form or another.

Too frequently, however, persons beginning a career in the stock market will grab at the most obvious part of the fundamental approach, that being the various financial statements, and build their entire case for or against selection of a company based solely on the current figures. This very often leads to conclusions favoring companies with a strong financial condition, particularly with no debt and large cash reserves. Now this is fine if one is seeking safety and insured dividend return. But the *fact* that a company has no debt and has large cash reserves is also an indication that the company is mature, and in fact, may be finding it difficult to put surplus funds to work.

Remember when we buy stocks we are not putting money in the bank. The whole basic theory of common stock investment *demands* the utilization of surplus funds in a more profitable manner than can be gained from placing your money in the bank or in bonds. Thus, a company with surplus cash reserves may be in exactly the same boat as the prospective buyer, that is, looking for a place to invest funds. Assuming they invest wisely, then the net effect may be to make the financial statement not as attractive as it appeared prior to their commitments, but in the long run will add to their profitability, which in the final analysis is why we invest.

Nothing I have said above should in any way be construed to mean that the financial statements of a company are unimportant or not worth studying. Quite the contrary. However, too often I find the fundamentalist resting his entire case strictly on the balance sheet.

If I were to ask you what things you would want to know about a business that you were considering purchasing in your

community, I believe that being a prudent man you might list
some of the factors below:

1. Assets-Liabilities	7. Licenses
2. Products	8. Patents
3. Management	9. Labor
4. Competition	10. Profits (past, present, projected)
5. Sales Organization	11. Research
6. Taxation	12. Government Regulations

Here are a dozen points I believe a prudent man should
investigate carefully if he is considering buying a small local
company. These same points are also of interest to a person
desiring to buy stock of any company, even though he may be
only a very minor stockholder.

But let's be realistic and appraise this type of approach in
terms of approximately 2,000 stocks listed on the New York
Stock Exchange, 1,000 listed on the American Stock Exchange
and better than 25,000 Over-the-Counter stocks traded regularly.
It should be obvious that the job of selection using all of the
above points is virtually impossible. Even the job of comparing
all the stocks in one industry group, based on the above considerations, while not impossible, would require considerable time
and effort.

Thus, in starting the selection process, I believe that we are
forced, at least in the initial stages, to try to find a short-cut
in lieu of answering all of the above considerations. Let us then
re-examine the list carefully and see if you can decide which
one or two of these fundamental considerations you consider to
be the most important and useful in comparing one stock with
another. If your answer is management, I ask you, "How do
you — living in San Francisco — appraise the management of a

company in New York or Texas or Florida or even in your own back yard?" If your answer is by their products, you are again partially correct if the product is in sufficient demand to sell at a profit.

A closer look at all of the factors will show that in one form or another all will be reflected slightly in the profits or the net earnings per share the company is capable of generating. Profits are the key reason that we risk our money. Thus a thorough study of management's ability to put the company's assets to work in the most profitable manner is of prime importance. The words "profits" and "earnings" will be considered as net figures and will be used interchangeably, as such, throughout the remainder of this book.

In the final analysis, we measure *management's* ability by the *profit* results it achieves as it sells its *product* in *competition* with similar or related products, the ability to *research* new products and protect their developments with *patents*, to meet the requirements of *government regulations* and *licensing* and to maintain orderly *labor* relations. This chain reflects itself in the net earnings of the company which become the single most important factor that we can use to begin our "short cut" to fundamental selection methods.

One important factor that I did not mention and one that will not necessarily reflect itself in the profitability of a company is the asset-liability concept of book value. The book value of a stock is determined by adding all the assets of a company (generally excluding intangibles), then deducting all debts and other liabilities, plus the liquidation price of preferred shares. This is divided by the number of common shares outstanding and the result is the book value per common share. The book value is not necessarily reflected in earnings because some types of businesses require huge capital assets and expenditures, but produce low profit returns. Others require only minimal assets to return substantially higher profits. In most every case I would choose the latter of these two alternatives. However I am usually amazed—in my discussions with fundamental analysts—at the continued preference for a company with a high book value. They will point out that the price of the stock is $15 per share and the book value is $30 per share, and even though the company was only able to earn $1.00 per share, they think it is a wonderful value because it is like buying a company for 50¢ on the dollar invested.

These same analysts will scoff at or claim absolutely no justification for the price of IBM, which sells in the $300 range and has a book value of approximately $75 per share and earns about $15 per share. Or Xerox, which sells in the $50 range and has a book value of approximately $25 per share but earns around $5 per share. I have never been able to understand the type of reasoning that does not allow one to realize that in the first case, it requires $30 of assets to produce $1.00 of profit and in the case of Xerox, $5.00 of assets to produce $3.00 of profit.

If we are truly going after our investment objective of making money, and if we understand that corporations are in theory designed to exist forever, not to be liquidated, then our quest is to find the most profitable ones in each time period. If you further realize that there are in actuality many companies whose price is below their book value, then those who express the desire to buy stock 50¢ on the dollar are saying that liquidating this company out of business may be the best way to make the company profitable. And it has been done.

There are obvious exceptions to this thinking, the most common being a "buy-out" by another company, particularly a natural resource type of company. But the principle is the same, that is, that somebody buys the assets, not the profitability.

In the table below are the companies included in the Dow Jones Industrial, Transportation and Utility Averages, with their book values and prices as of the end of 1975. See if you can determine any good conclusions regarding book value and the price of a stock.

INDUSTRIAL STOCKS

	Book Value	Price
Allied Chemical	$ 35	$ 34
Aluminum Co. of Amer.	$ 45	$ 39
American Brands	$ 22	$ 39
American Can	$ 42	$ 31
American Tel. & Tel.	$ 64	$ 51
Bethlehem Steel	$ 60	$ 34
Chrysler Corp.	$ 40	$ 11
Du Pont	$ 76	$127
Eastman Kodak	$ 23	$107
Esmark	$ 35	$ 32
Exxon	$ 38	$ 45
General Electric	$ 22	$ 47
General Foods	$ 19	$ 28
General Motors	$ 45	$ 58
Goodyear	$ 25	$ 22
Inco Ltd.	$ 19	$ 24
International Harvester	$ 54	$ 23
International Paper	$ 33	$ 58
Johns-Manville	$ 31	$ 24
Minnesota Mining	$ 16	$ 55
Owens-Illinois	$ 55	$ 52
Proctor & Gamble	$ 28	$ 90
Sears, Roebuck	$ 33	$ 65
Standard Oil of Calif.	$ 38	$ 30
Texaco	$ 32	$ 24
Union Carbide	$ 46	$ 61

	Book Value	Price
United Technologies	$ 28	$ 23
U. S. Steel	$ 59	$ 44
Westinghouse Electric	$ 22	$ 13
Woolworth	$ 32	$ 22

TRANSPORTATION STOCKS

American Airlines	$ 17	$ 9
Burlington Northern	$131	$ 34
Canadian Pacific	$ 26	$ 13
Chessie System	$ 70	$ 36
Consolidated Freightways	$ 12	$ 19
Eastern Airlines	$ 14	$ 5
McLean Trucking	$ 13	$ 19
Missouri Pacific	$ 23	$ 23
Norfolk & Western	$ 97	$ 21
Northwest Airlines	$ 29	$ 23
Pan American Airways	$ 6	$ 5
St. Louis - San Francisco	$ 83	$ 25
Santa Fe Industries	$ 60	$ 31
Seaboard Coastline Industries	$ 70	$ 22
Southern Pacific	$ 68	$ 30
Southern Railway	$ 43	$ 51
Transway International	$ 17	$ 18
Trans World Airlines	$ 18	$ 8
UAL	$ 30	$ 28
Union Pacific	$ 75	$ 78

UTILITY STOCKS

	Book Value	Price
American Electric Power	$ 22	$ 22
Cleveland Electric Illuminating	$ 29	$ 27
Columbia Gas System	$ 36	$ 23
Commonwealth Edison	$ 39	$ 30
Consolidated Edison of N. Y.	$ 36	$ 16

	Book Value	Price
Consolidated Natural Gas	$ 43	$ 25
Detroit Edison	$ 24	$ 14
Houston Industries	$ 31	$ 24
Niagara Mohawk Power	$ 17	$ 13
Pacific Gas & Electric	$ 28	$ 21
Panhandle Eastern Pipe Line	$ 40	$ 30
Peoples Gas	$ 49	$ 35
Philadelphia Electric Co.	$ 21	$ 16
Public Service Electric & Gas	$ 26	$ 18
Southern California Edison	$ 32	$ 21

Thus cutting through all the red tape, we logically conclude that the *most important fundamental consideration* we can make is a complete and thorough study of net earnings per share, the past *rate of change* for these earnings, the composition of earnings (direct from business or sale of assets), market price to earnings (P/E ratio), projected rate of change in earnings, taxable portion of earnings, earnings available for dividends, and earnings plowed back (cash flow). Now this may seem like a considerable effort, but if you will look at the graphs of Schering Plough (Page 61), Beatrice Foods (Page 127), Sears (Page 134), and Eckerd (Jack) (Page 155) and note the almost direct relationship between the rate of change in earnings and the rate of change in price, and also the rate of change in earnings and the rate of dividends paid out, I believe I can safely state that in the long pull, EARNINGS ARE THE SINGLE MOST IMPORTANT INFLUENCE ON THE PRICE MOVEMENT OF A STOCK.

There is another reason for the selection of earnings as the prime consideration for the study of the fundamental approach, and that is that earnings figures are usually readily available through condensed investment tables such as the Standard & Poor's Stock Guide or Moody's Handbook. While these stock

DESCRIPTION OF CHARTS

The majority of chart illustrations in this book cover a 12-year time span and are produced by Securities Research Co., a Division of United Business Service Co., 208 Newbury St., Boston, Mass. 02116. Below is a brief description of how to read these graphs. On the opposite page is a sample chart. Be sure to check the time period covered: monthly, weekly or daily.

PRICE: Monthly price ranges represented by the solid vertical bars show the highest and lowest point of each month's transactions. Crossbars indicate the monthly closing price. The price ranges are read from the scale at the RIGHT-hand side.

EARNINGS: Earnings are represented by the solid black line. Dots are to indicate when earnings are reported: quarterly, semi-annually or annually. Earnings are read from the LEFT-hand scale.

DIVIDENDS: Dividend lines represent the annual rate of interim dividend payments. The small circles show the month in which dividend payments are made. Dividends are read from the LEFT-hand scale.

RELATIVE
STRENGTH: This curve is based on the monthly closing price of each stock and its percentage relationship to the closing price of the Dow Jones Industrial Average. It thus indicates whether the stock has kept pace, outstripped or lagged behind the general market.

VOLUME: The number of thousands of shares traded each month is shown by vertical bars at the bottom of each chart.

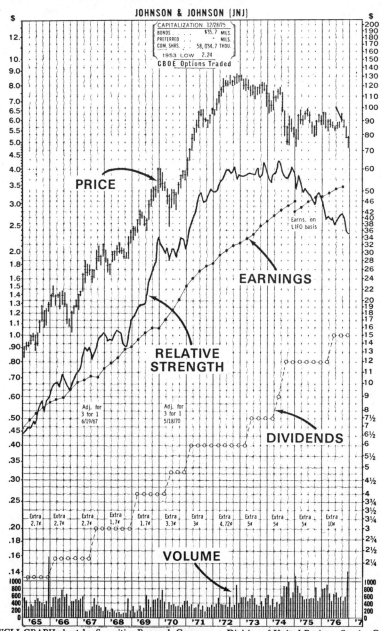

JOHNSON & JOHNSON (JNJ)

CAPITALIZATION 12/28/75
BONDS . . . $35.7 MILS.
PREFERRED . . — MILS.
COM. SHRS. . 58,034.7 THOU.
1953 LOW 2.24
CBOE Options Traded

PRICE

EARNINGS

Earns. on
LIFO basis

RELATIVE
STRENGTH

DIVIDENDS

Adj. for
3 for 1
6/19/67

Adj. for
3 for 1
5/18/70

| Extra 2.7¢ | Extra 2.7¢ | Extra 2.7¢ | Extra 1.7¢ | Extra 1.7¢ | Extra 3.3¢ | Extra 3¢ | Extra 4.72¢ | Extra 5¢ | Extra 5¢ | Extra 5¢ | Extra 10¢ |

VOLUME

'65 '66 '67 '68 '69 '70 '71 '72 '73 '74 '75 '76 '7

CYCLI-GRAPH chart by Securities Research Company, a Division of United Business Service Co.,
208 Newbury St., Boston, Mass. 02116

tables will not answer all the desired points mentioned above about earnings, they will give a good insight into the trend for earnings, the rate of change, dividend coverage, and—along with the current price—the current price/earnings ratio can be computed. As this information is reported in an identical manner for all the issues covered in these condensed tables, it makes cursory comparison possible. A more detailed study of the earnings should be made when and if the technical considerations discussed in the next chapter are in gear and as the final consideration prior to purchase. This more detailed study should include the other fundamental points mentioned at the beginning of this chapter.

TYPES OF EARNINGS CHANGE

As stated earlier, the rate of change in earnings is the single most important factor influencing the price movement of a stock. Thus, knowing the historical behavior pattern for a particular company becomes the best clue to what *may be anticipated* about future earnings. The typical patterns of earnings can be divided into approximately four main categories: recessive, income, growth and cyclical.

Recessive Earnings

Recessive type earnings, as the name implies, are earnings which over a long-long term period have been in fact declining. As the graph of Vendo on Page 57 clearly shows, while there may be a period of one to three years where earnings have advanced, over the 12-year span they must be viewed as declining. In most cases, this type of stock is to be avoided, as it is unlikely to accomplish the prime objective of making money. In fact, a stock with recessive earnings is very apt to have a recessive price trend, thus reversing the prime goal. Time is devoted briefly to this type of issue because so often newcomers will be attracted precisely to these issues because of their tendency to have a large dividend return. Some investors I have known

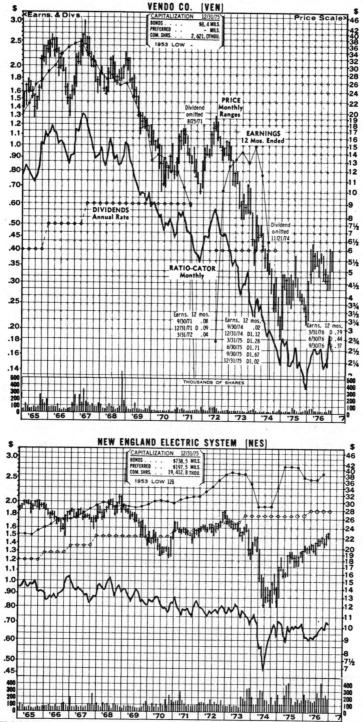

VENDO CO. (VEN)

Earns. & Divs.
Price Scale

CAPITALIZATION   12/31/75
BONDS . . . . $8. 4 MLS.
PREFERRED . .   - MLS.
COM. SHRS. . .   2, 621. OTHOU.

1953 LOW -

Dividend
omitted
8/25/71

PRICE
Monthly
Ranges

EARNINGS
12 Mos. Ended

DIVIDENDS
Annual Rate

Dividend
omitted
11/21/74

RATIO-CATOR
Monthly

Earns. 12 mos.		Earns. 12 mos.		Earns. 12 mos.	
9/30/71	.08	9/30/74	.02	3/31/76	D .79
12/31/71	D .09	12/31/74	D1.12	6/30/76	D .44
3/31/72	.04	3/31/75	D1.28	9/30/76	D .37
		6/30/75	D1.71		
		9/30/75	D1.67		
		12/31/75	D1.02		

THOUSANDS OF SHARES

'65 '66 '67 '68 '69 '70 '71 '72 '73 '74 '75 '76 '7

NEW ENGLAND ELECTRIC SYSTEM (NES)

$ $

CAPITALIZATION   12/31/75
BONDS . . . $738. 5 MLS.
PREFERRED . . $197. 5 MLS.
COM. SHRS. . .   19, 412. 8 THOU.

1953 LOW 12¼

'65 '66 '67 '68 '69 '70 '71 '72 '73 '74 '75 '76 '7

CYCLI-GRAPH chart by Securities Research Company, a Division of United Business Service Co.,
208 Newbury St., Boston, Mass. 02116

follow a selection method of simply going through some stock
lists or tables and selecting the issue having the highest yield.
Their next thought is usually to look up the rating of the company and if it should carry a "good" rating, then they will say
to themselves, "This is a good company; the dividend yield is
better than bank interest; I think this stock is a good buy." This
is the type of reasoning that typically leads to the purchase of
a recessive type issue. I would have no argument with the fact
that the company under consideration may have been, or in fact
still is, a "good company," but it is also certain that unless the
company changes its downward trend in earnings (profits) to
an uptrend, then eventually it will be in deep trouble, may even
go bankrupt. The capitalistic free enterprise economic system
is based on profits and if there are no profits, there is no company. This may take many years to occur, but why bet against
the trend unless you have very good reason to believe that these
profits will change shortly to an uptrend. A *hope* that things
may turn better before turning worse in a recessive issue is a
poor rationalization for receiving a high current dividend return. Too often the recessive earnings lead not only to a reduction in invested capital, but also to a reduced or omitted dividend, thus eliminating any possible justification for owning the
stock in the first place. Note the reduction and finally omission of dividends on the chart of Vendo.

Stocks showing recessive earnings tendencies should be considered with extreme caution. Purchases should be made only
when definite information of improved earnings is available and
where strong technical considerations also suggest buying. If
these conditions prevail, then it may be possible to profit by
buying into a recessive issue.

Income Earnings

A stock with *income* type earnings is illustrated by the graph
of New England Electric System on Page 57. Note the gradual
and steady improvement of the earnings over the last 12-year

span of time. There were some minor interruptions downward in the earnings trend, which were short-lived, before resumption of the upward pattern. Note the trend of the dividends for this issue; they were raised slightly every two or three years. Note also that the price movement of the stock has been relatively stable but gradually lower over this time span. Note that the major bottoms in the price movement of this stock tended to occur at the same time as the major bottoms in the general market occurred: 1966, 1970 and 1974. This fact will be important to our conservative-income blueprint in a later chapter.

This question must be asked of income type earnings: What creates such relative stability and what is the likelihood of a change for better or worse in the established trend? The answer is that the earnings of most income type issues are tied in some fashion to the population increase. In the case of New England Electric System, which is a regulated utility, other conditions may prevent maximum profits. But as regulations tend to be relatively similar in various geographical areas, the main difference becomes how fast the population is growing in these areas. Thus most income type issues will display steadily rising earnings trends.

Should a population explosion occur, such as that following World War II, then certain industries may experience rapid change in their earnings as this population wave affects their particular products or services, or until the wave is saturated and then returns to more traditional levels of growth. If for some reason the population trend generally, or in a specific area, begins to contract instead of expand, then those industries dependent on this expansion may be seriously affected.

Finally it should be noted in our example of New England Electric System that the dividend return was relatively high during the entire time period. During this same period the earnings for the stock rose at a rate of about 6% annually. This rate of appreciation must be distinguished from the next category of earnings which will be called growth earnings.

Growth Earnings

Growth type earnings are those, which in contrast to the income type above, are compounding at some higher rate and can be divided into two main classifications: *Leader* (or *Investment*) *Growth* trends typically show double or triple the rate of change in earnings as compared to income type issues, or approximately 10%-25%, and *Dynamic* (or *Speculative*) *Growth* issues will be two to three times greater than the investment growth issues, or 40% or higher.

To be a bit more specific in the distinction between the above terms, *leader growth* implies a company that in most investment circles would be considered the dominant leader within its respective industry, e.g., Coca Cola in the soft drink field, or Eastman Kodak in the photography field.

Investment growth implies a company with a high rating and usually a good earnings trend, but where dominant leadership is difficult to distinguish, e.g., in the drug industry.

Dynamic growth issues must have considerably higher rates of change in earnings than the above. They also typically have a *proven* product or service that appears to have a continuing large potential market. *Speculative growth* issues carry higher degrees of risk as their products or services may not yet be proven, but where the potential market, if proved, would be extremely profitable.

On Pages 61, 134 and 155 are graphic examples of each of the above, purposely exaggerated to more clearly illustrate. Notice the definite relationship between how fast earnings are moving up and how fast price is moving up. This leads to the obvious conclusion: "The stronger the earnings trend, the stronger the price trend." Notice how clearly this is illustrated by viewing the rates of change in earnings and prices on the various graphs. These graphs, which are produced by Securities Research Company in Boston, Mass., are without doubt one of the outstanding

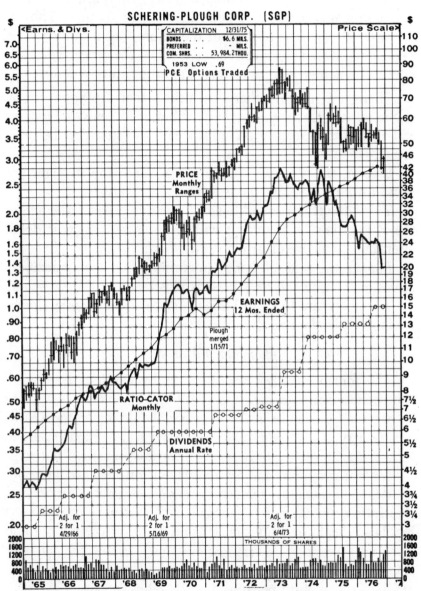

SCHERING-PLOUGH CORP. (SGP)

CYCLI-GRAPH chart by Securities Research Company, a Division of United Business Service Co., 208 Newbury St., Boston, Mass. 02116

tools investors may subscribe to in order to study past behavior
trends and the interrelationship of price, earnings, dividends,
P/E ratios, relative market performance and volume. They in
no way tell you anything about the future, but if you have no
understanding or perspective concerning the past, then it is
doubtful whether you can clearly appraise future potential.

There are several other conclusions that are apparent by
studying the three stock charts mentioned above. *First*, as
stated, the stronger the earnings trend, the stronger the price
trend.

Second, the stronger the earnings trend, the stronger the
trend for increased dividends at frequent intervals.

Third, the stronger and longer the earnings trend, the higher
the P/E ratio. This concept will be discussed in great detail
later, but should be clearly observed here.

Fourth, the rate of change in earnings has been amazingly
consistent during the time periods illustrated.

The above are the four basic conclusions that can be drawn
for income, leader and dynamic growth issues.

Cyclical Earnings

The fourth classification of stocks by earnings trends are
the *cyclical* issues, which are the most difficult and tricky to
work with. Cyclical issues, as the name should imply, have earnings that typically swing wildly in a cyclical fashion from one
time period to the next. Basically these are industries and companies that are more mature and whose fortunes are more dependent on general economic conditions. For purposes of
illustration, on Page 63 is a graph of Cerro Corporation, a
highly cyclical company engaged primarily in the mining and
smelting of copper. A very careful study of the interrelationship between earnings, P/E ratios, and dividends should be
made of this picture because it clearly illustrates that the conclusions concerning growth type and income type issues DO
NOT APPLY to cyclical issues. Non-recognition of this differ-

ence has cost investors many dollars in lost profits and will
continue to do so.

Beginning at the bottom of the cycle in 1953, note that the
price began to move up. It was almost six months later before
the reported earnings moved to the upside. (Remember that

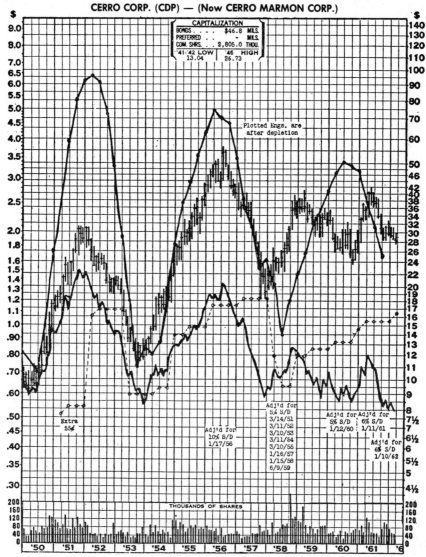

CERRO CORP. (CDP) — (Now CERRO MARMON CORP.)

CYCLI-GRAPH chart by Securities Research Company, a Division of United Business Service Co.,
208 Newbury St., Boston, Mass. 02116

earnings are always reported approximately three months behind the price due to quarterly reporting requirements.) Once the turn in earnings occurred they proceeded to move almost straight up from a low of 80¢ in 1954 to a high of $5.00 in the first quarter of 1956. The price moved steadily ahead of reported earnings during the same period, starting from a low of $11.00 per share in 1953 to a high of $56 per share in mid-1956. Assuming no other time period studied, this type of action certainly would qualify this stock as a dynamic growth issue. The earnings have risen 400% and the price almost 400% in a two and a half year period. To complicate matters further, the stock at the bottom in 1953 sold at 15 times current earnings and at the top in 1956 was selling at ten times earnings. This would appear to be in opposition to the basic conclusion concerning the P/E ratios of growth issues or in fact in opposition to simple logic, that is, having a high P/E ratio at the bottom and low P/E ratio at the top. Such are the facts of life when dealing with a cyclical type of stock.

If you will consider the whole cyclical swing from bottom to top and back to the bottom again, along with the psychological conditions that also prevail, you will see why I say that these are some of the trickiest stocks to deal with. Starting at the bottom (in most cases) we find a lot of bad news and gloom present; the price of the stock begins to move up even though the earnings are still moving down. It requires considerable courage to step in and buy under these conditions. By the time the company reports its first minor improvement in earnings, the price is approximately 100% off its bottom. It requires courage to buy stocks up 100% on only a minor increase in earnings. By the time the next earnings report is made, which shows a marked improvement, the stock is almost 200% from the bottom. The news and forecast are improving and, in fact, the company raises its dividend. By the time the peak is reached, the dividend has been raised twice and the earnings are in a fantastic uptrend, the P/E ratio is "cheap" and the news is exceedingly good. All conditions are present that make the uninitiated want to BUY the stock.

At the top, a sideways price action develops for about six to eight months while all the news is optimistic. Next the price begins to break into a downtrend and this is usually several months ahead of any downtrend in earnings. By the time the first downward change in earnings is detected, the stock is already approximately 20-30% below its peak price. The price continues to fall in the face of another minor decrease in earnings. The price drops all the way back to the $20 area and begins to move sideways. By now the earnings are also plunging and a dividend cut is made. The news is again black and the stock is now beginning to move slowly higher. Another dividend cut is made, earnings are still dropping and the P/E ratio is again quite high: these are the factors which must be viewed as opportunity when buying a cyclical type issue. What would your reaction be if your investment advisor should call you on the phone and say, "Mr. Client, I think you should consider Cerro Corporation for purchase. The price of the stock has dropped from $56 a share to $19.50; the earnings have dropped from $5.00 a share to 95¢; the dividend has been cut from $1.25 to 65¢ and the price-earnings ratio has gone up from 10 times earnings to 20 times current earnings. This is a real buy."

Think clearly what your most likely reaction would be. Probably anything but rushing to buy such an issue. As a matter of fact, you might decide it was time to change investment advisors! Reverse the above considerations and see how easy— psychologically—it would be to buy the same issue at the top. But these considerations are the facts of investment life when considering the purchase or sale of a cyclical type industry or individual stock. They may be summarized as follows:

At the bottom of the cyclical swing:
   1. Earnings are falling.
   2. Dividend may be cut or omitted.

3. High P/E ratio.

4. News generally bad.

5. Price movement has stopped falling and has moved sideways for four to six months.

At *the top* of a cyclical swing:

1. Earnings are moving straight up.

2. Dividends being raised.

3. Low P/E ratio.

4. News generally excellent.

5. Price has been moving sideways for four to six months.

The importance of a clear understanding of these typically cyclical stocks cannot be overemphasized as approximately two-thirds of all companies from which our selection will be made are cyclical to some degree. These companies include some of the oldest, largest, best-known and highest rated companies in the country. Below are listed the major industry groups that typically have cyclical earnings characteristics:

Airlines	Meat Packing
Aluminum	Mining and Smelting
Autos	Rail Equipment
Auto Parts	Rails
Building Materials	Rubber
Copper	Shipbuilding
Farm Equipment	Shipping
Machine Tools	Steel
Machinery	Textiles

You will note how many blue chip companies will be included in the groups mentioned above.

It is also important to understand that a cyclical issue, properly purchased and properly sold, can be as profitable as some of the most outstanding growth issues. But the key issue involved here is that the typical cyclical upswing lasts approximately two to three years and then retraces a substantial portion

—if not all—of the up move. To avoid the downswing by selling is to be understood as part of the objective from the day the first purchase is made. A growth issue may, on the other hand, continue its upward movement with only minor set backs, usually in conjunction with general market swings, for ten years or longer. A cyclical stock is not the type to be put in the lock box and forgotten; a true growth issue is.

By now it should be obvious that a clear understanding o. earnings and their typical movement patterns is one of the most important fundamental factors that we have for analytical consideration. It should also be obvious that we can get a substantial change in the price of the stock without necessarily a similar change in the earnings trend, particularly as applied to income and growth type issues. This variation is due to the second most important fundamental variable that we can study, that is, price /earnings ratios.

Price/Earnings Ratios

The P/E ratio is determined by dividing the earnings into the price, and is essentially a psychological variable of how investors are currently appraising a particular stock or industry. There is a great amount of incorrect information written and expounded concerning P/E ratios, the most common of which is to set some absolute standard or norm for all stocks, such as 15 to one, and then arbitrarily concluding that stocks selling below 15 times earnings are bargains and at 25 times earnings are too high. This type of reasoning unfortunately has led investors to some poor profit conclusions. For example, during the past decade, some of the best investment grade growth stocks have seldom or never sold as low as 15 times earnings, and some of the dynamic growth stocks, e.g., IBM and Xerox, have been bargains when they sold as low as 28 to 30 times earnings. Thus, following an arbritrary figure as a guide to what is high or low would have kept investors from owning two of the most outstanding money makers.

There are some other outstanding growth issues, such as Overseas Shipbuilding Group, that rarely sell as high as 15 times earnings. A more detailed study of the important fundamental factors reveals that each stock and industry group has typically established some traditionally high and low P/E ratio valuations. Therefore, individual valuations have far greater importance to selection of a particular stock than some arbitrary yardstick applied to all issues. Determining what these traditionally high and low P/E values are can be done in several different ways. The easiest is to subscribe to a service such as "Trendline's,"* which gives you these levels and categorizes stocks by groups, so that by a brief check of other issues in the same group an estimate of the industry P/E ratio can be gained. As an example, the drug industry is typically a high P/E ratio group, with the average low valuation about 18 times earnings and the high about 36 times earnings.

Another method of determining this traditionally high-low P/E valuation is by securing a Standard & Poor's report, available in most all brokerage offices. On the back of this report you will find statistical tables covering the highlights of financial data for approximately ten years. On the far right hand side you will see a column indicating the highest and lowest P/E multiple for the past ten years. Make an average of the lows for the past ten years and then for the past five years. Giving slightly more weight to the past five years, you should be able to get a good idea as to the customary P/E ratio for an individual issue.

A note of caution about this approach: the major variable here is earnings first and P/E ratio second. A stock that today is selling close to its traditionally low P/E ratio may not be a good bargain if its earnings in fact are headed lower. Devoting some extra time and research in an attempt to secure a projection of next year's earnings may prove very profitable. A stock whose earnings are projected level, or higher, should contain relatively small downside risk when selling at or near its tradi-

*Trendline's Current Market Perspectives, published by Trendline Corp., New York, New York.

tionally low P/E ratio. Another point of caution applies to *cyclical* earnings: it becomes almost impossible to establish traditional levels for cyclical issues. Thus the high-low P/E valuations concept is applied best to industries which display a consistent upward trend in earnings.

Sale of Assets, Taxes and Cash Flow

Sometimes a stock will appear completely out of line with its currently reported earnings and P/E valuation, giving the appearance of being an exceptional bargain. A more detailed study of these reported earnings will usually reveal one of the three possibilities listed below:

1. Reported earnings *included* the sale of some asset which is a non-recurring factor and thus is not truly from current operations. This will typically make the stock look "cheap." Subtract out that portion of non-operational and non-recurring earnings; then the P/E valuation is likely to be more in line with the group.

2. Another important consideration is what amount of current earnings are *taxed*, as tax laws allow companies to carry forward losses that occurred in previous years. A company that is reporting very good earnings and selling at what appears to be an extremely low P/E ratio must be checked to determine what tax rates are being applied. If the company is paying taxes on all of its earnings then you may have found a bargain that has been overlooked. More often, however, you are likely to find that the company has had several years of deficits and finally its earnings are in the profit column. In this case, it may not be paying any—or reduced—corporate taxes, and thus the currently stated earnings must be reduced as if the taxes had been paid before making a comparison of P/E valuations with stocks in similar lines. As an example, a company that is operating profitably will pay corporate taxes of 50%. A company that brings forward a tax loss may, in the first year of profitability, pay no tax, the second year pay a 20% tax and the third year

pay 40%. Finally, after all the tax loss is used up, it will be taxed at the 50% rate. During the time a tax loss carry forward is being applied, the P/E valuation of the stock will appear "cheap" on a current basis. This often explains the wide difference between stocks within the same group.

3. Another concept that has become widely used is a method of comparing profitability known as cash flow. Simply stated, cash flow is the reported earnings plus the amount of depletion, depreciation and research that the company is allowed to write off. Adding these factors together, then, the cash flow is going to be somewhat higher than the reported net earnings. As these funds are not truly operating expenses but more of a reserve for future contingencies, then a company that is generating a high cash flow is stacking up some substantial reserves which, if wisely used, can add substantially to their future profits and growth.

Therefore a company that looks very high in terms of P/E valuation may in fact be found to have the highest cash flow ratio in the group. A high cash flow factor has in recent years usually been considered a healthy condition, for the company is able to finance its growth and expansion without additional dilution through equity financing or burdensome borrowing.

These then are some of the variables of reported earnings that must be taken into consideration when appraising earnings and P/E ratios as a method of selecting a stock to purchase. The most important factor obviously is what the earnings will do in the future. *Projected earnings* are not easy to make or secure and this is why the stock market is not an exact science and why even the best of analysts will differ in their opinions. The first step in gauging future earnings is by some insight into their previously established record. A company with a history of adding to their earnings at approximately 3% to 4% per year is going to require some major change in its character, or nature of operations, in order to change this pattern to any degree. Thus traditional P/E valuations become the major variable.

A company whose history is 20% growth and steady, e.g., Schering-Plough, is probably making every effort to maintain that rate of growth. Again the primary variable is P/E ratio. As

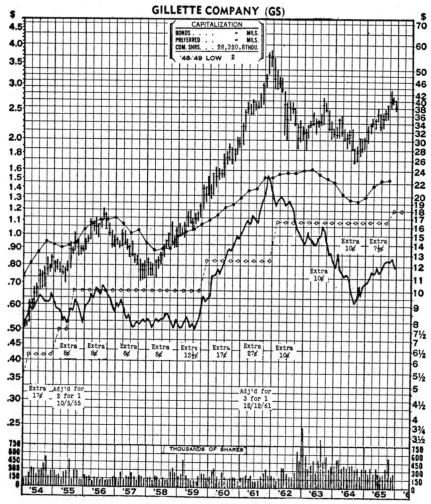

CYCLI-GRAPH chart by Securities Research Company, a Division of United Business Service Co., 208 Newbury St., Boston, Mass. 02116

the graph on Page 61 indicates, they have done an excellent job for many years. Careful reading of any statement by management as to projections for the coming year is important; always watch reported quarterly earnings to detect any slowing of traditional earnings growth rates. Watching developments of similar products that may seriously affect this type of company is also important, as the picture of Gillette on Page 71 reveals. With the advent and instant popularity of the stainless steel razor blade, Gillette—whose revenues were 70% derived from the sale of regular blades—was certain to be adversely affected. Note from the graph that the price of the stock was abnormally weak and earnings were still moving higher. This is often a clue to "danger ahead" for earnings.

Stocks showing 40% earnings growth or greater must be viewed carefully as to products, competition and market saturation, as this rate of change is extremely difficult to continue for more than three to five years. But it has been done and will be done again in the future. Stocks having this potential will typically sell at extremely high P/E multiples which should not be surprising. If the average stock's rate of earnings growth is 10% per year, then a company that grows four times faster than the average should, logically, carry a P/E valuation considerably greater than that of the average. Yet few investors I have encountered will appraise issues in this fashion. They will typically tend to say that the average P/E multiple is 16:1 and very high at 30:1 and completely non-justifiable or ridiculous at 50:1. Yet some of the outstanding growth issues of the past two decades have sold at times well in excess of 50 times earnings.

One final word about the concept of P/E ratios. Between 1950 and 1964 we were in a period of generally rising P/E ratios for the average stock. However, the upward trend was broken in late 1964, and was followed by a period of generally declining P/E ratios. This means it should pay investors

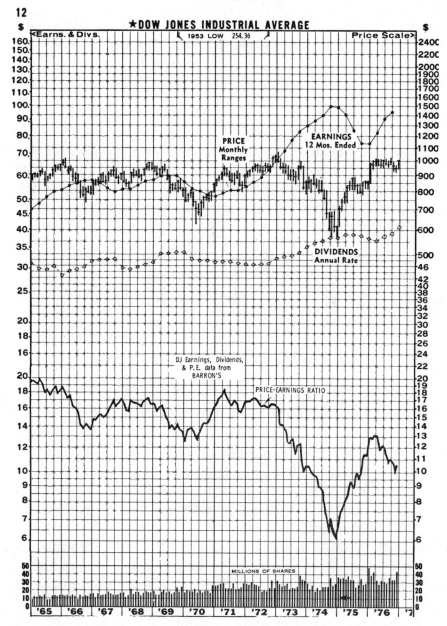

Source: Securities Research Co., a Division of United Business Service Co., 208 Newbury St., Boston, Mass. 02116

to make estimates of individual P/E ratios conservatively until we again see P/E ratios rising. Recently, the average stock has been selling at 10 to 13 times earnings or less, a far cry from the 23 times earnings of the early Sixties.

Summary

In summary, then, earnings become the single most important factor that we can take from the fundamental approach as a method of selection of individual securities, the conclusion being that earnings (profits) are the most influencing fundamental factor on the price movement of a stock, and that:

1. The more stable the earnings, the more stable the price.
2. The wider fluctuating the earnings, the wider the fluctuations in the price.
3. The greater the rate of change in earnings, the greater the rate of change in price.

The second most important fundamental factor is the P/E multiple, from which we draw the following conclusions:

1. Each income and growth type issue traditionally establishes high and low P/E multiples. (These should be viewed as approximations and should be reviewed occasionally to detect whether these valuations are changing.)
2. A stock selling at its traditionally low P/E valuation and whose earnings are projected to continue higher during the coming fiscal year is usually at or close to its bottom and affords very small downside risk, thus becoming a candidate for purchase.
3. Stocks selling at their traditionally high P/E valuation are subject to greater downside risk than upside potential even though projected earnings may be up.

4. Earnings must be watched closely to detect any change in their traditional rates of growth.

5. The above conclusions DO NOT APPLY to stocks with highly cyclical earnings.

We now move on to the technical approach for the selection of groups and individual stocks. In establishing investor blueprints in later chapters, we shall utilize the above conclusions along with various technical and psychological factors.

TECHNICAL APPROACH

The technical approach, in contrast to the fundamental approach, deals with the price of the stock, the volume (or number of shares that were traded) and the date on which the transactions occur. Technical analysts believe that while certainly a study of the company is important, the *final* appraisal by investors will be first detected in the price movement of the stock itself. Thus the technical analyst bases his entire study on price movement, volume and date. Other technical analysts will go so far as to state that price, volume and date are the only *true facts* in the stock market with which to deal, as fundamental factors are actually not facts but the opinions of management.

While there may be some merit in this thinking, it still demands appraisal of the products or services of the companies—which are facts—by investors to determine the long range potential. Thus, by nature, the technical approach is typically shorter in time emphasis than is the fundamental. In either case it should be understood that the fundamentalist always asks "why" or "what" is happening to make the price move up or down and will not usually take any definite action until he finds out.

The technician will take action based on the fact that the price *is* moving up on the assumption that when the reasons are announced they will prove favorable, or, in the case of falling prices, that when the reasons behind the fall are announced they will prove to be unfavorable. The technical student works on the clear premise that price movement *anticipates* events and acts accordingly. This premise has such an excellent batting average that all fundamentalists should take some notes as we discuss the methods of selection from the technical approach.

Relative Strength

The basic and best tool to be gained from the technical approach to selection is known as "relative strength." This concept has been called by many names but is no more or less than the relative price movement between one stock or industry group and some broad group of stocks used to represent the average movement, such as the Dow Jones Industrial Average or the Standard & Poor's 500. The mathematics of this computation can be accomplished in several ways, the easiest being to divide the Standard & Poor's 500 Average into a stock's closing price on Friday of each week:

$$\text{S \& P 500} \overline{\smash{\big)}\ \text{price of stock}} \quad \text{Relative Strength}$$

While the resultant figure by itself is meaningless, the direction in which these numbers are moving becomes extremely important. Assume that after several weeks of computations the figures are basically unchanged, or if plotted on a graph, would give a sideways appearance such as below:

Relative Strength Curve—Neutral

The interpretation is that this particular stock is moving approximately the same as the Standard & Poor's Average, percentage-wise. The price of this stock may in fact be up or down as a sideways movement of the relative strength does not mean the price of the issue is necessarily sideways, but is percentage-wise approximately equal to the movement of the Average. The most important conclusion here is that the supply-demand factors for the particular issue approximate that of the average issue and have no special dynamics of their own.

Now, assume that these relative strength figures are in fact declining and again if put on a graph would show a downward trend:

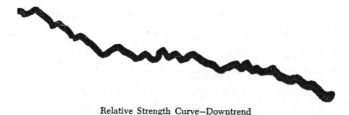

Relative Strength Curve—Downtrend

The interpretation is that this stock is doing worse than the average stock. Is the actual price of this stock downward? Not necessarily. The price may in fact be rising even while its relative performance compared to the average is declining. Why? Investors are not willing to pay as much for this second stock as for the first. Why?

Now assume that the relative strength figures are moving higher and on our hypothetical graph would appear something like this:

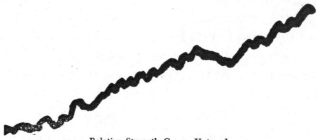

Relative Strength Curve—Uptrend

The most important interpretation here is that investors, for some reason, are willing to pay more for this third stock than for the "average" first stock and considerably more than for the second issue. Again, why? The best and only conclusion that can be drawn from this type of analysis is that in the case of number one, the supply-demand factors are about in balance, whereas in case number two there were a greater number of sellers than buyers (or no buyers). However, in the third case the demand was greater and investors are willing to pay more for this stock. The exact reason *cannot* be ascertained from looking at some line on a graph or a set of statistical tables. But think carefully about this entire concept. What better tool could we develop to point us in the right direction than a tool which tells us—at any given moment—where the demand appears the greatest. Again it must be pointed out that a rising relative strength curve does not necessarily mean rising price, but it can mean that the price is dropping *less* than the average stock, thus still displaying greater demand. The interpretation remains the same. A rising relative strength curve and falling price trend is an outstanding BUY indicator. This occurred with General Motors in the general market break of May, 1962, and Boeing and Motorola in June, 1965.

Relative strength is the most important *tool* we can take from the technical approach and it does no more nor less than to focus our attention in the right direction at the right time in history. While I believe it is best categorized as a "selection tool" it obviously is also an important timing tool. To make a clear distinction between the concept of selection vs. timing, those tools that are most helpful in determining "what to buy" are called selection tools. The tools that are most useful in answering "when," or the price at which to place the order, are called timing tools. At the moment, we are discussing selection tools.

Comparative Analysis

Before going further into our study of selection it becomes necessary to introduce two concepts that underscore the importance of selection. The first I shall call *comparative* analysis, which means making comparisons between industry groups and then between individual stocks within the group. When you invest your capital you are at all times seeking the greatest amount of safety versus potential appreciation rewards. You are at all times saying in effect, "What risk am I willing to assume to possibly achieve 50%, 100%, 200%, 1,000% appreciation?" To do this you must compare issues. All too often an investor will come into my office and say, "Lockheed is a good stock. Don't you think I should buy some?"

My answer for years has always rather stunned the questioner, as I would say, "Lockheed is a good stock in relation to what?" Then they would usually tell me about the assets of Lockheed, that the company is a "big" company, they have a new government contract, etc. Now, certainly Lockheed is a "good" company as are the vast majority we have to select from. The real question is: Is Lockheed the best candidate for purchase when *compared* with Boeing, McDonnell Douglas, Martin-Marietta, Rohr Corp., etc.?

In order to determine which candidate is best for purchase demands comparisons. The first comparison is to determine if the Aircraft-Missile group is the best group to have some funds invested in at this moment in time, or if some other group looks better.

Answering the comparative question leads to the true answer investors are seeking. "I think that the Aircraft and Missiles Group is one of the best groups to be investing in and that the best candidate to meet my personal risk vs. potential requirements is Lockheed Aircraft Corp." It should be obvious that this latter statement is made after an investor has made some definite comparisons and it is extremely logical. Yet, the vast majority of investors that I have had contact with will go no further than to say, "Is this a good company? I think I'll buy some."

Trend Analysis

The second concept is known as "trend analysis." What is a trend? The dictionary says a trend is "to have or take a general course or direction." This definition applies to many areas of business and to our professional lives. In recent years, we have witnessed a trend from big cars to small cars, a trend towards filter cigarettes, etc. Women often refer to a trend as a "fad," especially in reference to clothing. The politicians refer to the trend of public opinion and businessmen may be struggling to reverse a downward trend in sales or profits. In the stock market, when we discuss the trend in the price of a stock, the trend in the relative strength, the trend in earnings or dividends, we are simply discussing the direction in which these factors are going. In discussing the direction of a trend there are only three possible alternatives:

1. Up.
2. Down.
3. Sideways or Neutral.

The method employed to determine the direction of a trend can be rather complicated, but for the moment, let's assume that if given a set of figures or a graph that you could make a rough appraisal as to the trend. Your first conclusion is likely to be your best; don't attempt to make things more difficult. If the figures are tending upward, then the trend is up.

Now assume for a moment that you are looking at the weekly closing price of three different stock issues:

Stock A: 10, 10½, 10½, 12, 11½, 11, 13½, 15, 14½.
Stock B: 25, 24½, 24¾, 25¼, 24½, 25, 24¾.
Stock C: 75, 76, 75½, 73½, 74, 71½, 72, 70½.

With no other information than the above figures, which stock do you think has the highest probability of its price moving higher in the weeks ahead? The answer is Stock A, and is the basis of all stock market trend analysis: that a trend once established tends to continue in the same direction.

Back in the mid-thirties, Alfred Cowles of the Cowles Commission, after some very exhaustive study of stock price trends, concluded that the probabilities were approximately 65% that if a stock price trend was up, it would continue up. Think of what a valuable tool it is to know what the trend is before investing in a particular stock. Further refinement of the above axiom is required, and that is: Trends tend to continue in the same direction — until clearly reversed. Don't be dismayed by this further complication. The reversal of a trend is our opportunity or hazard and forms a timing consideration, discussed in the next chapter. What is important to understand is that while there are hourly, daily and weekly trends, when discussing selection of a stock we are discussing a trend that averages approximately two and a half years, and if it is an uptrend, it may be anywhere from a minor percentage gain to possibly several hundred percent during this time span.

The goal of trend analysis is best expressed in an "S" curve:

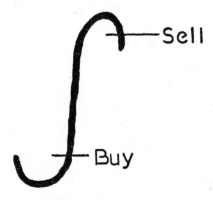

What is desired is to buy into a new uptrend as soon as a clearcut decision is made that the trend is definitely up. This may mean anywhere from 10% to 30% or more off the bottom and is considered by the technical analyst as the insurance he pays to have the 65% probability factor on his side. Assuming the trend does in fact continue up, the next point is to look for some change in the upward trend that may be followed by a then clear reversal to the downside. This may require selling 10% to 30% or more off the top.

Now, obviously if you are dealing with an income type of stock that typically only goes up an average of 10% a year, then it is going to be pretty tough to buy 30% off the bottom and sell 30% from the top. So you are going to have to hit the bottoms and tops much more closely to profit from such a concept as trend analysis. More typically, however, taking a growth issue or a cyclical issue in an uptrend, you may be amazed how many will go up 100% to 300% or more in the next two and a half year period. Thus, using the "S" curve, assume you buy at $15 per share. The stock subsequently reaches a high of $60, but you wait to be sure the trend has reversed and sell out in the $50 area. This is known as riding the middle ground and it takes the bulk of the percentage profits out of the swing and does not allow you to stay around to see how far down is down in the next downtrend. When I discuss the blueprints in later chapters this concept will come into focus, but it becomes important to understand the value of trend analysis, how it works, and then to see how we make use of it.

Understanding and acting upon this "trend continuation" concept is the heart of technical analysis. It is not altogether as easy to apply as it may appear, because there is always the creeping doubt that the trend has already advanced too far to allow for much greater upside potential. This is the downfall of most investors, as they say to themselves, "I missed it," and again begin to look for the stock that hasn't moved up so far or in fact may not truly be in an uptrend. Typically this is a natural habit as most investors will constantly search for "bargains." Bargains in their minds are those issues selling at or close to their lows for the past year or so. In most cases these stocks by our trend concept are in downtrends, placing the odds 65% against making a profit shortly after the time of purchase. If the bargain purchased is a high quality issue in a basic and proven industry, in time the trend may turn favorable, but it could be months or years later.

The continuing task of making money with your investment funds is not a simple one. It requires hard work and study and decisions based on the best available evidence at the time of purchase. To deliberately step into a downtrend where the odds of success are definitely against you is foolhardy. If you step into a situation where your best calculations suggest success, and then for some reason the trend does not continue or even reverses, this is a very legitimate error. This again requires your best emotional control, first to recognize that you may have erred, and second, to take corrective action in order to minimize losses. Never forget that the investor who places as many factors as possible on his side is still only going to have a 65% to 75% batting average. This still leaves a 25% - 35% possibility of erroneous calculations to be reckoned with. In the long run, investors who clearly understand these probability factors and learn to expect 35% errors as part of the total investment job, will make money. The difference in being very successful and moderately successful is how fast you learn to recognize an error and take action to minimize your loss. The investor who is slow in taking profits and fast in taking losses in time will be very rich. *The safest stock is one in which you have a big cushion of profit.*

Understanding these various factors of comparative analysis and trend analysis clearly is important as we now return to development of our most important technical *selection* tool: relative strength.

Let us now proceed with the task of selection. Our objective is to develop a method of selecting several issues for purchase from literally thousands of candidates. We have also learned that to do a good job requires some comparison and finally a decision as to what is the best investment at any given moment.

It should be obvious that we cannot compare some 30,000 stocks in order to arrive at conclusions, but it is possible to break down many stocks into similar or identical industries. Below is a breakdown of industry groups which contains about 90 divisions.

Industry Groups

Agricultural Implements
Air Conditioning
Aerospace & Aircraft
Aerospace Equipment
Airlines
Aluminum
Amusements
Apparel
Apparel Stores
Auto Materials
Autos
Autos, Truck & Trailer
Beverages, Soft
Biscuits, Bread, Cake
Broadcasting
Building Materials
Can Manufacturing
Cement
Cereals & Grain
Chemicals
Clocks & Watches
Coal & Coke
Confectionery
Cosmetics
Dairy Products
Dental Supplies
Department Stores
Drugs

Drug Chains
Electric Products
Electronics
Engineering & Heavy Equip.
Fertilizer
Finance Companies
Floor Covering
Food, Misc. Products
Furniture
Glass
Holding Companies
Household Products
Instruments & Controls
Insurance
Investment Trusts
Iron Ore
Liquor & Beer
Lumber & Wood Products
Machine Tools
Machinery, Construction
Machinery, General
Mail Order
Meat Packing
Metals, Specialty
Metal Products, Misc.
Mining, Copper
Mining, Gold & Silver
Mining, Misc.

Motion Pictures
Natural Gas
Office Equipment
Oil Production
Oil Refining
Oil Well Supply
Optical Products
Paints
Paper
Paper Containers
Photo & Camera Equipment
Printing Machinery
Publishing
Radio & TV
Railroads
Railway Equipment
Razors
Real Estate
Refractory Products

Refrigeration & Heating
Restaurants & Hotels
Savings & Loan
Shipbuilding
Shoe Manufacturing
Soaps & Cleaners
Steamship Lines
Steel
Sugar Prod. & Refining
Sulphur
Supermarkets
Telephone & Telegraph
Textiles
Tires & Rubber
Tobacco
Transportation, Misc.
Utilities
Variety Stores
Vending Machines

Not all stocks can be placed into an industry group classification, but approximately 90% of them can and this becomes the starting point in our search for the issues we desire to purchase. While it may be impossible to compare 30,000 individual issues, it is very possible to compare the relative performance of 90 groups once or twice each month. Our basic tool is relative strength and this can be calculated for a group by using five to eight stocks in the same or similar industries and developing an average price for the group, then comparing the price movement for the group with that of the Standard & Poor's 500 Stock Average. I strongly do *not* recommend that you make all the computations necessary to develop the various group averages or the relative strength figures; this data can be purchased from any one of several excellent sources and I am a strong believer that investors should purchase statistical data and spend their time on interpretation and decisions. On Page 87 is a comparative study done of the relative strength curves for 24 leading industry groups at the beginning of 1963, approximately three months past the October, 1962, major bottom.

Stop for a moment and study this picture carefully. Remember that you are looking at relative strength curves, not price curves. Now, to get the full value from these pages, you must be willing to make decisions. Take a separate sheet of paper and write down the industry groups that appear to be *clearly* in a relative strength uptrend. Now another decision is necessary. Select the five industries whose uptrend is the strongest, and finally, arrange the five in their order of strength.

Whether you realize it or not, you have just made three extremely important decisions at a moment's glance. You have selected five industry groups where for some reason the demand factors are greater than for the average stock. Or, phrasing it slightly differently, the wonderful focus tool of relative strength has rapidly and accurately brought five industry groups to your attention by telling you that for some reason investors are willing to pay more for (or sell less of) the automobile stocks than the steel stocks. Why? At this point, you do not know why, only that further study of each group is required.

The next step in the selection process is to write down the names of all the individual companies that should be included in each of these five groups. *Now,* the decision to be made is which one of these *individual stocks* is the strongest. Next, which company has both strength and quality or is the highest rated, which shows the strength and which pays the largest dividend. Notice that these latter questions are beginning to bring into the selection process the fundamental considerations of quality and dividends. Within each group, using no more than the concept of relative strength, it is possible to make rapid comparative analysis to determine the strongest, the strongest with quality, and the strongest with the biggest dividend. The most important rule in applying relative strength is that *the strong tend to get stronger and the strongest tend to remain the strongest.*

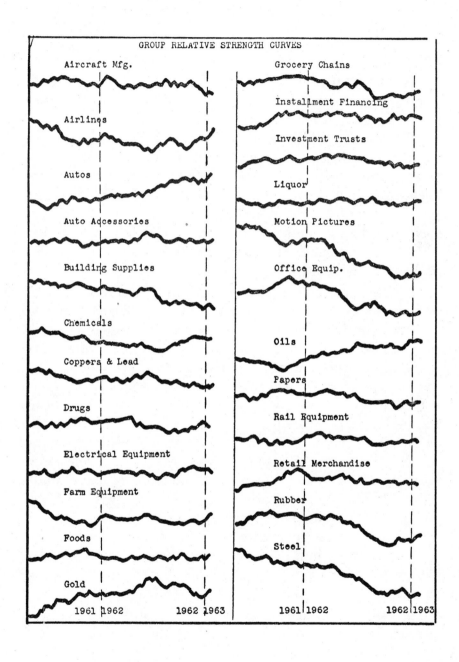

GROUP RELATIVE STRENGTH CURVES

The strongest relative strength stock, however, may not necessarily have the attributes of quality and large yield, but by this process it is possible to satisfy the various requirements of the individual's desired blueprint.

The stock displaying the strongest relative strength is the stock likely to appreciate the most from bottom to top. I repeat: the strong tend to get stronger.

Determining which is the relative strength leader can be accomplished in one of several ways. Buy a statistical service which makes such computations, e.g., Investors Research or Trendex, or buy a chart service that has relative strength curves such as Securities Research Company charts. Note how much each stock in a group has appreciated during a certain period. The strongest relative strength issue is the one that is up the most, or down the least, as the case may be.

It should be obvious that our steps thus far have been an attempt to rapidly reduce this vast array of 30,000 stocks to something workable and this has been accomplished by breaking 90% of the stocks into approximately 90 groups. Then, utilizing group relative strength as our "focus tool," we have selected five or ten industries for further investigation. This additional survey again utilized the relative strength concept to compare the performance of individual issues, and then we select two or three within each group for more detailed study.

The above process has reduced some 30,000 possible candidates to approximately 30 good candidates for more study. Now, without doubt, any serious-minded investor is capable of doing a great deal more fundamental study about these 30 stocks in order to select five for purchase.

The first step in the fundamental process is to determine if the stocks under consideration are classified as growth, cyclical, or income stocks.

Second, make an earnings study of previous, present and projected earnings and apply fundamental rules discussed in the previous chapter.

Third, make the P/E multiple study as discussed earlier.

Now, having applied the three steps of rapid fundamental analysis, the list of 30 candidates may now only contain ten stocks, but *never* eliminate the *strongest* relative strength stock in any group until the final exhaustive study says to do so.

The final study of the remaining stocks should be in considerably more detail, and for the first time, attempt to answer *why* this stock and group is in greater demand by investors. The key fundamental word you must keep in your mind at all times is *change*. We do not profit greatly by static conditions. You may receive a better than average dividend and possibly relatively steady appreciation, but I repeat, you will *not* profit greatly from static conditions. Thus as you delve into the more minute details of a company, such as are listed on Page 48, keep in mind what factors have changed or are changing in this company that have attracted an unusual demand for the stock. Often times a company may have had a *change* in management, or a *change* in its financial structure by securing a big loan. Watch for a *change* in name, particularly where the new name is closely identified with major products, e.g., South Penn Oil to Pennzoil.

A company whose financial structure looked terrible in past years, almost to the point of bankruptcy, but currently has a strong relative strength trend and at the moment no concrete evidence of better earnings, is often a good candidate for solid fundamental improvement. If big money has confidence in management, they will begin to buy anticipating a *change* for the better.

In this final study you are searching for the stock which is likely to show the greatest improvement in earnings. Thus, a company that has a satisfactory record of earnings may not be the best price appreciation candidate, because, to a company with deficit earnings, any improvement will cause a greater percentage change. Never forget that a company with potentially outstanding products may run in the red for years as it plows funds back into research and development for the product. But as the payoff approaches, the stock will begin to move up ahead of any actual reported earnings, maybe six months to a year in advance.

In this final countdown of fundamental considerations, keep in mind that you are trying to answer the question, *why?* and this becomes very important to the long term investor. It is possible to make profits based solely on the trend analysis of the relative strength, but there is little confidence gained by looking at comparative statistical tables or charts. Attempting to find more concrete reasons is primarily for the purpose of giving you, the investor, the confidence to get on the trend and then stay with it. Without the confidence of fundamental reasons why a group or individual stock is moving, investors tend to become faint-hearted and grab an early profit, or panic on the first minor decline. Finding the precise reason is by no means easy or even possible, but definitely requires a great amount of independent thought, which starts by asking questions:

1. What factors about this industry group have changed?
2. Is that change minor or major?
3. If major change, is it likely to affect only one stock or the whole industry group?
4. How long may the improvement be expected to last?
5. Will the change create new or different markets or customers?

Apply some of these thoughts to the airline industry in late 1962 or early 1963. They were in fact, at that moment, one of the five leading industry groups from a relative strength standpoint. Beginning a fundamental rundown was almost frightening as the picture revealed a highly cyclical industry, constantly moving from feast to famine over the previous 15 to 20 years.

Most of the companies were in debt up to their eyebrows, and most of them had declining earnings and had reduced dividends in recent months as they went even further into debt to buy new jet planes. The industry was anything but glamorous and I remember many investor comments to the effect that "I wouldn't own an airline stock if you gave it to me." There weren't many tip sheets telling investors to buy airlines, or if they did it was a rather guarded or hedged recommendation. And the news from the companies was none too good, e.g., the strike of flight engineers and low occupancy rates, and always government regulation. Needless to say, people were not rushing to invest their money in the airlines.

But—big as life—the group was among the leading five industry groups coming off the bottom of October, 1962. Why? Through all the above, the *change* that was beginning to occur was that *jet* airliners had been just long enough in service in a few of the major lines to revolutionize the whole pattern of airline operations. Speed was the big factor. The same airplane could fly several trips between New York and San Francisco each day. Crews could make a round trip the same day. The speed tended to stimulate more flying as businessmen found it profitable to meet with clients or customers. The planes themselves, while costing more originally, carried more passengers, operated on cheaper fuel, and required a minimum of maintenance. These were all big changes that were beginning to filter down from the experience tables of the earlier jets in use. It was a trend that would eventually affect all airlines, even down to the puddle jumper runs.

It was likely to be a several-year trend just allowing time to manufacture the planes themselves. The companies which acquired the first jets benefited the most and therefore were among the earliest relative strength leaders. These are some of the factors that possibly explain why this industry was one of the leading industries in early 1963.

Three years and many jet miles later, these early possibilities or suppositions were very obvious facts. In the meantime, the average airline stock was up almost 500% since those opening days of 1963.

Could you have asked for a better selection tool than that of group relative strength to clearly *focus* your attention in the right direction at the right time?

To better illustrate how the comparison of some of the individual airline stocks' relative strength curves looked at the beginning of 1963, see the study on Page 93. Note that the early relative strength leaders were: (1) Delta Airlines, (2) National Airlines, (3) Pan-American in the approximate order of visual strength. It is interesting to note that from the beginning of 1963 to the end of 1965, Delta appreciated 500%, Pan-American 300%, and National 600%, but American Airlines, while carrying a higher rating and paying a higher dividend, moved only 250%.

These relative strength comparison studies are the most valuable selection tools an investor can employ. Again, I highly recommend the purchase of the data and then you can concentrate your efforts on interpretations and decisions.

PSYCHOLOGICAL APPROACH

The psychological approach to selection and timing is the most illusive and yet probably one of the most important areas for study and research. The psychological approach deals more with you, the investor, than any actual facts about the companies or even the trends for the stocks. Fortunately or unfortunately, all factors for appraisal are working at the same moment in time and cannot be separated as they are in these pages.

The heart of the psychological approach is simply that in order for stocks to truly be on the bargain counter, the prevailing news at the moment is likely to be *bad*. This condition is a prerequisite for big money accumulation.

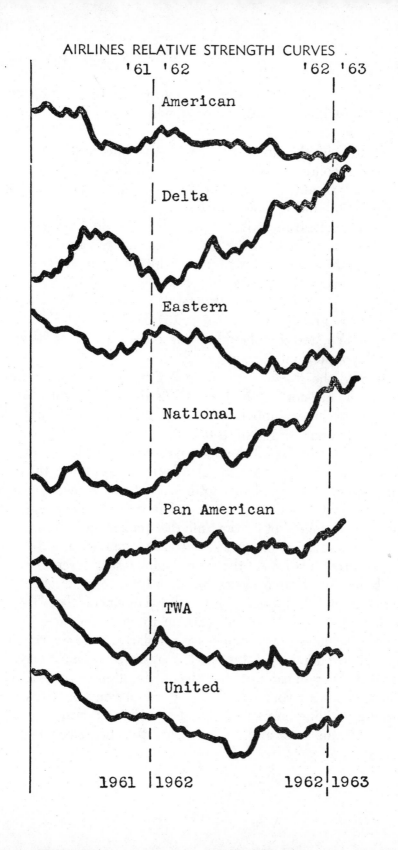

AIRLINES RELATIVE STRENGTH CURVES

'61 '62   '62 '63

American

Delta

Eastern

National

Pan American

TWA

United

1961 1962   1962 1963

On the other hand, for big money to sell their positions they must find willing and ready buyers, which typically means good news items.

Obviously, this approach is a relative one, and it demands emotional contrariness on the part of the investor. At the bottom of a typical downswing for an individual stock, when solid fundamental and technical factors say now is the time to buy, news items cloud the possible purchase with doubt. It is at this point in time, when the risk is the least, that the average investor will adopt the philosophy of "wait and see." If the price should drop slightly lower, he places his order 50% below the prevailing price, convinced that he will "steal" the stock a little later. If the price moves up 10% to 15%, he follows the "I missed it" approach, and if it should return to the recent low, he won't miss the opportunity again.

Should the stock continue up 20% to 30%, it now becomes "too high" or "not worth chasing." As the stock climbs 50% to 100%, it becomes "unbelievable." As the stock soars past the 150% mark, the attitude shifts to "it's going up forever."

Early in this period the news was negative. Slowly, ever so slowly, the problems and the clouds began to part as the company in fact didn't go bankrupt but is actually showing a slight improvement in earnings. Few people paid much attention to the early change, but by the time the stock is up 150% or more, it is amazing how many tip sheets are recommending the issue as the "growth stock" of the year. A new research report on the stock may be secured by sending in a little coupon. About this time our mythical average investor is convinced that "the sky is the limit"; he throws all caution to the wind and "jumps aboard." Believe me, it happens as regularly as the sun rises and sets. There comes a point where the pressure to "jump" becomes so great that you can truly feel the old heart pound as you place your order with your broker. For those of you who have been making a killing on paper without actually investing, put some money in the kitty and see how hard that heart of yours will pound.

If you don't feel any loss of emotional control on the upside, then let's take you through the downslide. Once aboard and in the swim of things with the crowd, our mythical stock continues up and within days you have a profit, maybe as much as 10% to 20%. You say to yourself, "There's nothing to it; what have I been missing all my life? I had better hock my house; I could retire in a few years at this rate."

Suddenly, and without sending you an advance telegram, the stock takes a sharp dip, bringing it back to about what you originally paid for it. The news is all great; the trend for the industry is a "lead pipe cinch to go higher" over the next few years. Nobody is worried about this minor "technical correction." Besides that, some of the big fellows down at the brokerage office, the ones who come in every day and watch the tape, are buying more.

After a sideways trading range of several weeks, the stock breaks lower, now below your original purchase price. Convinced that the stock must now be a "better value" or "buy" at lower prices, our typical investor buys more or at least forms the opinion that all is well and that "this is a good stock so I'll just hang on until I can *get out even*."

Now the general market is falling also. There is muffled talk in the board rooms about "1929." The price of the stock is falling every day now. The news continues to worsen. Due to "heavy fog" or some reason (principally, the Accounting Department) the new quarterly earnings report shows a worse loss than the first and now there is a question as to whether there will be enough profit to cover the current dividend.

In the meantime, the international news is worsening, the general market is CRASHING, and at an emergency meeting the Board of Directors decides to reduce, postpone, or omit the current dividend. By now our investor's heart is not only pounding, but he experiences a rather ache-all-over feeling of tense muscles. Make no mistake, this is the emotion of FEAR, and the best way to relieve this strain is to SELL and say "to hell with it. I'll salvage what I can and put it in the bank." If this hasn't happened to you, then you are oblivious to what is happening or you are dead.

The ability to act contrary to the prevailing mass opinion is known as the "art of contrary opinion." It is by no means easy. It requires extreme emotional control when every emotion in your body is telling you to buy when you should be selling and to sell when you should be buying. Recognizing this and acting intelligently in opposition to these emotions is a prime requisite for making continued profits in the stock market.

Chapter VI

TIMING THE PURCHASE OR SALE
OF INDIVIDUAL SECURITIES

The next area of study is the technical approach to timing (as opposed to the technical approach to selection discussed earlier). This approach deals primarily with the price history of the stock itself, which is best understood by looking at a graph or chart of some type. The best graph service that I have found is produced by Securities Research Company in Boston, Mass., which publishes quarterly cycli-graphs displaying a 12-year history of monthly price action. My experience has shown that the longer term charts are the best for selection considerations and the shorter term for more precise timing. This is often a mistake made by the tyro technical analyst; he makes his study with daily charts and seldom works backward to check the very long perspective. However, by beginning this study with a 12-year perspective, the current price levels and ratios come immediately into focus with the past. A chart is valuable only in that it tells you of the past and how that past is related to the present. The future depends on the current trend, and charts become invaluable tools in recognizing a change in trend in the price of the stock or in the relative strength. Thus, a chart study of price movement becomes the technical analyst's primary timing tool for answering the question *when* to buy.

There are several timing methods by which one can recognize the change in the price trend, the most common being

97

trendlines or moving averages. A moving average is made by first establishing a simple average for a fixed time period (such as 10 or 20 weeks), then dropping the earliest price and adding in the most recent price for the new week. If the current price is above the 20-week average, then the trend is considered to be up. If the current price is below the 20-week moving average, the price trend is down. While this may be an oversimplification of the use of moving averages, it is the primary concept, and is well covered by Joseph Granville in his book, "A Strategy of Daily Stock Market Timing for Maximum Profits."

Trendlines

Maintaining moving averages requires a tremendous amount of work on the part of the individual investor, and therefore I recommend the purchase of this data from services such as Trendline or R. W. Mansfield Co. However, I consider the trendline concept to be as good as, or better than, the moving averages concept and therefore we will study trendlines in greater depth.

An upward price trend as applicable to stocks can be defined as the price movement that is continually making higher highs and higher lows—in price. A downtrend is when the price is making lower highs and lower lows. Graphically, it would look like this:

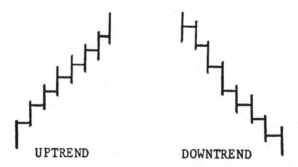

UPTREND   DOWNTREND

As long as this phenomenon continues, there becomes no question or doubt about the trend. Unfortunately, stock prices don't move in such well-defined trends indefinitely, thus being able to recognize a shift in trend becomes important. Here again, however, we must more clearly define a shift of trend over a several years' period, or a daily period.

As this entire book is designed for long term investors, I shall confine this study to the major shifts which occur over some years and the intermediate shifts which will tend to alert you to possible major shifts. The primary tool used to establish a shift in trend is known as a *trendline*.

Trendlines are drawn by connecting as many peak prices as possible in the case of descending general patterns as in the graph of Chrysler Corp. on Page 100. Note that the major trend for Chrysler between 1953 and 1963 was basically down, but the trendline had clearly broken to the upside by late 1962 in the $15 price area. Now note a combination of factors: group relative strength said to look at autos; individual relative strength said Chrysler was very strong. Fundamentals at that time revealed a major change in management and a reshaping of the company's policies; and finally, a nine-year price downtrend is broken in the $15 price range, thus establishing a definite price area to watch closely and take action accordingly. You should also note from the picture of Chrysler that a trendline drawn on the relative strength curve broke to the upside almost three months *ahead* of the price trend break.

In the case of uptrends, the trendline is drawn by connecting as many bottoms as possible. You are looking for any major shift in the established trend, as shown in the graphs of Reynolds Tobacco on Pages 101 and 102.

Major trendlines are established over several years' duration and have far greater significance than any shorter period of time. Or, saying it another way, the most valid trendline is the one covering the longest period of time. Thus, I strongly recommend that for *buying* considerations a monthly graph showing the longest time period possible is desirable. However, when the issue is already owned, and because stocks decline more

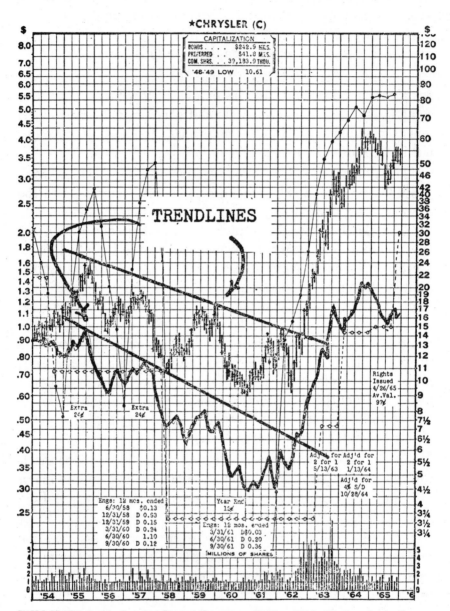

★CHRYSLER (C)

TRENDLINES

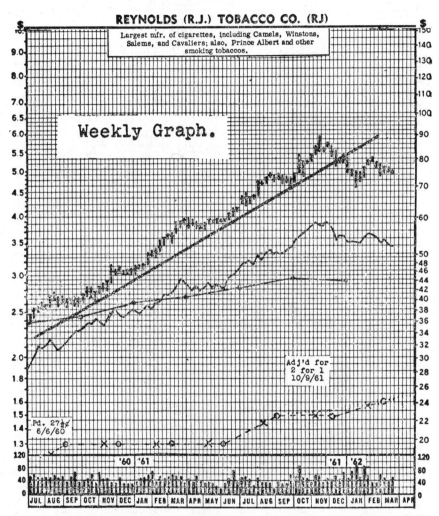

REYNOLDS (R.J.) TOBACCO CO. (RJ)

Largest mfr. of cigarettes, including Camels, Winstons, Salems, and Cavaliers; also, Prince Albert and other smoking tobaccos.

Weekly Graph.

Adj'd for 2 for 1 10/9/61

Pd. 27½¢ 6/6/60

THREE-TREND security chart by Securities Research Company, a Division of United Business Service Co., 208 Newbury St., Boston, Mass. 02116

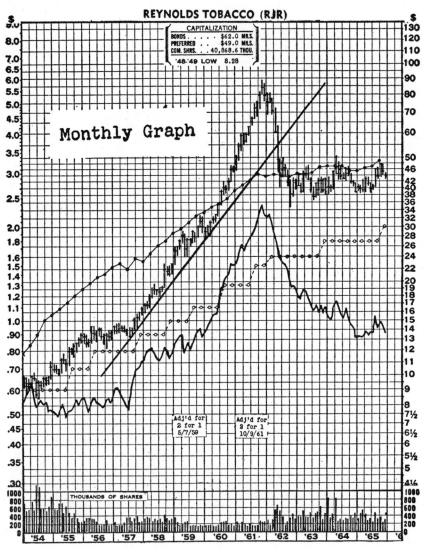

CYCLI-GRAPH chart by Securities Research Company, a Division of United Business Service Co., 208 Newbury St., Boston, Mass. 02116

rapidly than they advance, I suggest a weekly graph covering approximately a two-year span. Notice the difference in price in Reynolds Tobacco by looking at the weekly instead of the monthly chart. A clear alert of a shift in trend showed on the weekly graph for Reynolds as it broke through the $80 area. It would not have registered a major long-long term sell signal until breaking the $55 area.

Trendlines are not magic; they have no meaning except to alert the investor to a possible shift in trend and to establish an actual price zone where this is likely to occur. If all other factors suggest buying, then the break of the price trendline to the upside is the *final clincher.*

In the case of selling, the break of the price below the upward trendline is likely to be one of the *earliest* warning signals of danger ahead, and requires some definite decision on the part of the investor.

Many times there will be false breaks of the trendline. Therefore, it pays long term investors to move slowly but to be alerted to possible changes which may affect their holdings.

Note, as I stated above, the price break above a descending trendline was the clincher to a "buy" situation, meaning it was one of the last roadblocks or considerations, *not* the first. However, a break of the price below the trendline may be one of the *first* clues of trouble, and hence it is of greater importance.

One of the other best guides to selling is that of the traditionally high P/E ratios discussed earlier. In either case, this whole business is based on probabilities and if the evidence begins to mount in favor of a downtrend, don't make the most common of all errors in the stock market and ask, "How far down is down?" Do as the skydivers do and "hit the silk."

Volume

Volume is another of the major areas in the study of technical analysis. There have been many theories put forth concerning the interpretation of volume, and while some of these theories may have merit, in most cases it requires a task force of computers to keep the data current and, as such, it becomes highly impractical for utilization by most investors. This is by no means to imply that volume is unimportant, but that volume is only another tool among many and its importance should not be blown out of its proper perspective.

First of all, volume is the total number of shares that change hands on a daily, weekly or monthly basis, in any one individual stock. Volume is *not* comparable between different issues because each company has a different number of shares outstanding. Thus, it is not possible to compare the volume of shares traded in General Electric 225 million shares outstanding) with that of Emerson Electric (57 million shares outstanding). It should be obvious from this illustration that General Electric may be often found among the ten most actively traded stocks, whereas Emerson Electric would seldom have a chance to make this "hit parade" of volume leaders. *What is important is the comparison of the volume of each stock by itself.*

Without too much effort, it is possible to roughly establish what the approximately "normal" trading volume is for most listed stocks. By normal is meant the rough average in some given time period such as 30 days to several months. As volume is always changing slightly, a normal volume in early 1977 may not be applicable in late 1978. "Normal volume" should be used only as a guide to help distinguish exceptionally abnormal volume.

If the rough normal volume can be established for each stock, then what would the advent of extremely large volume possibly portend? The answer is possible *change*. This being the case, then, a stock displaying abnormally large volume should be watched closely for change in whatever pattern or trend has been occurring.

Thus, we quite logically find *big volume* typically occurring at the beginning of a new trend or at the end of an old one, or to make it even more clear, big volume in individual stocks typically occurs at the tops and bottoms of their major cycles. (Note carefully that this differs from the general market pattern of volume, which has peak volume occurring at the halfway point in the major swing.)

"Big volume" should be defined as three times or more greater than the previous "norm." Thus, if the price trend of a stock has advanced substantially for a considerable time period, and big volume begins to develop, then the advancing price trend must be watched closely for possible change. Quite often the change that will occur will be to halt the advance and a new sideways or neutral trend will begin. Where the price trend has been falling and big volume begins to occur, then the bottom is probably not far off. Here again the trend is likely to shift from down to neutral, with the price moving sideways for possibly several months or sometimes even years. "V" bottoms do occur from time to time, but 90% of the time a sideways trend will follow a downtrend. On the opposite end—at the top —however, the sideways movement may prove to be very short before either a resumption of the uptrend occurs, or a new downtrend gets underway. Big volume then becomes the EARLY WARNING SYSTEM of a possible change in trend, and, used in conjunction with other fundamental and technical factors, can be a useful timing tool for both buying and selling.

As an example, review the chart of Chrysler on Page 100. Note the change in volume pattern that occurred in late 1962. Also note the extreme volume peak that occurred in late 1963. This latter volume spike stalled the advance and shifted the trend to neutral for almost eight months, before resuming to the upside.

Notice the huge change in the volume relationships that occurred close to the bottom of the General Electric drop in early 1961. Big volume typically occurs in actually four critical points: it stops a downtrend, stops an uptrend, starts an uptrend, and starts a downtrend.

Remember that big volume is 65% of the time the best early warning system of change and that the immediate trend for any stock displaying unusually large volume must be suspect—this may be for the better or worse. The price area where the big volume is occurring should be clearly marked or made note of. Should the price of the issue subsequently drop 30% or more from its highest point and substantially below the area in which big volume occurred, then on a rally back to the lower area where such volume developed, a sale should be made or at least a protective stop loss placed.

Time Study

The final tool of technical analysis is *time*. Our tax laws were such that large money investors were required to hold their stocks for a minimum period of six months* in order to profit fully. This simple fact of life is what typically creates the two intermediate buy points per year in the general market as we discussed in earlier chapters. Make no mistake about the fact that big money, buying and selling individual stocks, is what makes the price go up or down. This is not to imply that all money is going to be shifting at the end of the six month period, but that better than 50% of the time—six months after a stock begins a major advance— it will take a substantial correction and move sideways, possibly for several months.

You must ask yourself the question, "What advantage is there to holding a stock longer than six months?" The answer is that it is going higher during the next six month period, and possibly for several years. Assume a stock has been moving sideways for several years, having declined from an earlier high point 50% above the current price. Big volume begins to develop as the price of the stock comes to life. Six months later the stock has appreciated 100% from the first sign of big volume out of the sideways movement. Almost six months to the day after this first big volume occurred, you can expect a dip of some type to

*Changes in the tax laws stipulate a holding period of nine months in 1977 and one year thereafter to qualify for long term capital gains treatment.

develop. This occurs as those who think that a 100% profit in six months is sufficient, or who believe their money may work harder in another stock, sell out. After the initial run, it becomes more difficult to distinguish these six month time periods. Quite often what happens after a six month run is that the issue will take a dip in price of 10% to 20% and then go dormant or sideways for the next four to six months before resuming an uptrend. As the average length of time for a long term upswing is approximately two years, stocks which have been in an uptrend for two years or more should be viewed cautiously as time may be running out. In most cases, you will find that after a two year uptrend, the issue is likely to be selling close to its traditionally high price/earnings ratio. Thus, it becomes a candidate for selling.

Percentage Dips

Before leaving the technical study, some discussion of the "normal" percentage dips that a stock will make during a strong advancing trend is important. While the high and low for the month—as seen in most graph illustrations in this book—make the price movement appear almost straight up for several years, this is not typical of the day to day action that we must live with. On Page 108 is a chart of Natomas that illustrates quite well the more typical *daily* price movement of a strong uptrend.

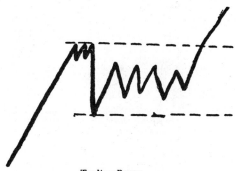

Trading Range

Note that basically the pattern is one of several steadily advancing days, followed by one to three sideways at high

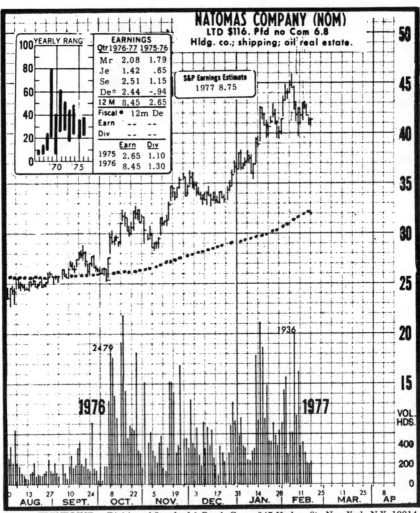

prices, then a sharp break lasting about three to five days, then a bounce back about half the distance of the drop. Then typically following is a sideways movement which is termed a "trading range."

This is what I call the normal price pattern of a stock moving in a strong uptrend. As long as each of these daily or weekly percentage dips stays above the lows of the previous one, and then within a thirty to sixty day period makes a new high, the upward trend should be considered intact and there is no cause for concern. If you wish to know *why* this is the typical order of an upward price pattern, remember we are dealing with the forces of supply and demand activated by people. The "trading range" areas are where the supply and demand factors are approximately in balance. This balance may last for only a few moments or possibly for years, but if the stock is truly in an uptrend, this equilibrium price will seldom last over several weeks. Thus, having used up all the supply in one particular trading range area, and with the demand continuing to be strong, the price begins to move higher to attract someone into selling. This typically occurs by a fast run to a new high point, maybe 10% to 15% above the previous high. The reason for this fast run is that at each price level some people are "thinking" about buying the stock and some are "thinking" about selling. The buyers, noting that the stock is beginning to "break out" of its trading range on the upside, will no longer postpone their decision to buy as they realize the trend is up and the stock is likely to move higher. Potential sellers who did not sell while in the trading range and who note that the stock is on the up move again, will typically delay selling, hoping for a better price or for the first sign of a downswing. Thus, for a moment (approximately as the stock "breaks out") there becomes an excess of demand and no supply, which accounts for the rapid rise. Now, as potential sellers first see the stock price stall or fall back slightly, they will begin rapidly to sell, creating a fast dip after a sharp runup. As the price dips, those potential buyers that missed the last trading range begin to buy and another trading range is formed as the tug-of-war between supply and demand again repeats itself.

Approximately the same reasoning applies to a downtrend situation except that from a balance in the trading range there is now an excess supply and the price drops sharply lower for several days. Potential buyers, thinking that the stock is a better bargain at lower prices, will rush to buy, again making the stock rally back approximately half the fallen distance or more and here again a new trading range is established. There does not necessarily have to be a specific fundamental reason for these relatively minor changes in price; the reason is, simply, that the short term forces of supply and demand are adjusting themselves to the long term prevailing trend.

What is important is to be able to distinguish what constitutes the "normal" dip pattern of stocks from an "abnormal" dip pattern, which may be a warning signal of change. I have found that the percentage dips depend on the price of the stock, and the table below indicates the approximately normal percentage price dips of these minor swings:

Price of Stock	Normal Price Dip*
$ 0 - $10	30 - 50%
$10 - $20	20 - 30%
$20 - $40	15 - 20%
$40 - $80	10 - 15%
$80 - up	8 - 12%

*Measured from most recent peak price.

Note that these price reversals should be considered normal for a stock in a strong uptrend and that over a year or two a major upswing may go up several hundred percent. Note, too, that the higher the price the less the percentage dip it will make, but that the point count will be greater. Should a stock in the $40 to $80 price bracket dip 20% to 25%, this puts up an automatic "caution flag," not necessarily a sell signal, because the odds heavily favor a retracement of at least 50% of this dip.

By the same token, a stock that makes dips less than the normal must be viewed as a possible *powerhouse*, indicating a tremendous demand even at steadily advancing prices.

Always remember, however, the basic axiom is sell rallies, buy dips. This concept may tend to trigger a discussion of the merits of buying breakouts or buying dips. After many battle scars, I have resolved this question by the following procedure:

> Buy power (thus breakouts) 30 to 60 days following a general market intermediate bottom, then shift to buying dips until the next intermediate bottom.

While this concept may have a poorer batting average than others discussed in this book, it should help to save the investor the agonizing experience of buying a large percentage of false breakouts.

Summary of Technical Factors

Technical analysis offers investors several important tools that should not be ignored. Below is a brief summary of these tools and where they are most helpful.

Selection Tools

RELATIVE STRENGTH:
1. Best used as a selection tool to focus the investor's attention on those industry groups outperforming the average stock.
2. Used as a rapid comparison tool to determine the strongest stock within an industry group.

Timing Tools

TRENDS:
Probability factor 65% that an existing trend will continue in the same direction.

TRENDLINES:

A timing tool to help recognize any shifts in trends. May be used in conjunction with the price movement or relative strength curves. Breaks in trendlines are typically late to register buy or sell signals.

VOLUME:

Big or unusual volume in a particular stock is often the earliest warning that the trend may be at its end, or a new one is about to begin.

TIME:

While major trends tend to last an average of two years, important price dips often occur six months after the first volume thrust into a new uptrend.

Chapter VII

DRAFTING YOUR BLUEPRINT

Now, having built a framework of reference concerning the best features of the three possible analytical approaches, it becomes important that each be interrelated in its natural state because only in theory can they be dissected. Also, there are a great number of variations that investors may employ in the management of their own portfolios. This chapter stresses the "order of things" and elaborates on several variations that may be employed.

We started our study of the stock market by gaining a very long-long term perspective. Then we examined long term cycles lasting one to three years and finally, we examined the 60 to 120 day intermediate swings that occur regularly in the general mass market movement. No attempt was made to refine further the day-to-day ripples for the general market because this book is written primarily for investors, not traders.

Working from a long term perspective to a shorter term perspective is one of the first important points in the drafting of a blueprint. However, far greater *emphasis* should be placed on the current data and the future change possibilities. But examination of the long term reveals the entire history and allows for greater emphasis on *major* change, rather than minor change. As an example, a stock price breaking into new high ground for the first time in five years is a more significant occurrence than making a new high for a single week or year. Similarly, breaking of a 12-year trendline should be considered of greater significance than breaking a two-year trend.

The goal of a successful investment philosophy is to gather as many positive factors as possible in order to maximize the odds of success. The next step is to determine which factors do have an effect and which are the most important and deserve greater emphasis. The major factors that will have a direct bearing on the odds of success are:

1. Relative strength trend for an individual stock.
2. Earnings rate of change for an individual stock.
3. Relative strength trend of the industry group containing #1.
4. Price trends for an individual stock and group.
5. General market trend, both intermediate and long term.

The factors listed above are in the relative order of importance and require more explanation for emphasis.

Relative Strength Trend
for Individual Stock

If I had to select one tool at the exclusion of all others, I would select the relative strength tool. Without knowing the name of the company, its products, its earnings, its rating, its dividend (and if my investment life depended on such a decision), I would bet on the relative strength tool for my success. I don't think that I can say more to emphasize this point.

Rate of Change in Earnings

The second tool in the order of importance is a record of the previous rate of change in earnings. The best estimates or projections for the coming year and the next three years for the earnings should be included, as well as the traditionally high and low P/E ratios and the current P/E ratio.

It would be necessary at this stage to know the major product or service producing the earnings in order to truly arrive at a judgment about projected future growth. The major point in this consideration is that a company having exceptional potential gains in earnings, meaning a substantial rate of change between 50% to 100% per year for several years, is likely to be in a strong relative strength uptrend and less likely to be influenced by other factors listed below.

Group Relative Strength

The third factor in importance is having the entire industry in an upward trend. This does not mean that every stock within the group must be up, but the majority. A question might be asked here: Do stocks actually move up or down as a group? The answer is definitely yes. This may not happen on the exact same day but over the average two-year cycle the positive or negative factors that affect one or more are likely to affect most all of the issues.

Is it absolutely essential to have the group trend up before buying an individual stock within the group? The answer is no, but again it provides a margin of safety that many investors are anxious to have on their side. As noted above, if a stock has exceptionally strong potential earnings and a strong relative strength factor, it will move independently of any group trend. An outstanding recent example of this has been the Xerox Corp. More common, however, is one individual issue that is making gains of 10% to 20% in earnings while the balance of the groups' earnings are down or sideways. This stock will definitely tend to be affected by a downward or sluggish group movement. It may in fact drop in price even though steady earning improvements are being made. This always baffles the strict fundamentalist. Or it may move up slightly as the group moves downward; the result is still a slowing of the upward progress primarily attributable to unfavorable group psychology.

Typically, there are one or possibly two issues that are the "advance guard" of a new group uptrend. For example, Boeing Co. in the Aircraft Manufacturing group turned up early in 1964. These "early leaders" are usually the ones which have made the greatest improvement in their fundamental position during the time the group was psychologically out of favor. This advance leader (or leaders) will often lead the turn six to 12 months ahead of much activity in the balance of the group. Following the group very carefully after the *advance leader* has clearly shown up can be very profitable, like a "crystal ball," as rotation within the group occurs. While there can be many variations, a good rotational pattern is the *quality* stocks leading the turn, the secondary issues next, and finally the speculative • issues last.

Price Trend of Individual Issues and Groups

Obviously, in order to make money, the price of the stock must advance. This may sound a little redundant in relation to the number one factor of upward relative strength, but remember the price of a stock can be falling and still have an up relative strength factor. The up relative strength factor is suggesting, however, that any downswing or sideways movement in price will be temporary and an upward price will shortly ensue.

General Market Trends

Finally, and least important, the general market trends have a definite influence on the odds of success. Strangely, this is rather a double-barrelled influence and is primarily psychological but is a factor which must be reckoned with. No doubt you have heard the expression "you can't buy the Dow Jones Industrial Average." The implication here being "so why even consider it." Now, of course, those who make such statements are correct in the bare facts of the case, but these same people are likely to explain why they sold out completely and put their money in the bank by saying, "The market looks too high," or "I thought the market was headed much lower." The "market" they are referring to in most every case is the Dow Jones Industrial Average. Few people bother to discuss the number of issues advancing or declining which is really where your odds of success are calculated. Even the pros who clearly understand the interworkings of the market will be influenced by what is happening to the Dow Jones Industrial Average because they understand the psychological approach to the market is as important as any other.

Here is what typically happens. The Dow Jones Industrial Average is the most widely published measurement of what the movement of the average stock has been throughout the day. Thus radio and television reporters, along with many newspaper writers, report this Average daily and usually the total volume of shares traded. Now I doubt that there is one out of 100 brokers' representatives who can tell you what stocks comprise the Dow Jones Industrial Average or what divisor is used to arrive at the current Average, to say nothing about how much the various reporters know. But the psychological influence of listening to your favorite radio program during the day—which is interrupted occasionally to report what the Dow Jones Industrial Average is doing—or of tuning in the major TV news in the evening and again learning what happened to this Average is very, very real.

Here is how it works: if the Average is going up with only minor daily setbacks, then there is no cause for concern, or any great motivation to do any buying. As a matter of fact, it becomes a nice evening's "pacifier" to learn each day that things in the financial world are not collapsing.

So, the Average has little effect as long as stocks are generally rising. But let's see what happens when the world of the Dow Jones Industrial Average goes into reverse gear and heads down. The first evening reports of setback are typically met with a brief grin from the easy chair and a glance at the wife with a brief comment, "I knew it was about time for a dip." The next several evenings the procedure is repeated without much alarm as the losses are relatively small. Then the evening comes when the loss is much more substantial and the reporter is saying it is the biggest drop in the last five months. Mr. GrimJaw from his armchair decides at this time he had better check his holdings to see how well they're doing.

The next day was a bad day to check on his stocks, however, because of an important golf match that he had planned for several days. Returning home just in time to learn that the Dow Jones Industrial Average was up for the day, he was glad he had played golf, and why get upset? He owns "good stocks." The following evening the Dow Jones Industrial Average is again down sharply. This is followed by five more evenings of falling Dow Jones Industrial Average without any specific news events to explain the drop. By now Mr. GrimJaw decides to finally see his broker and find out "what the score is." His broker can't explain the reason for the dip but points out that most of the issues he holds have been acting well and a couple have even moved higher. Fortified with the assurance that, after all, he holds "good stocks" and no "experts" are predicting a major crash, he returns home to greet the new bull swing.

He becomes totally unnerved when, during the next two weeks, the Dow Jones Industrial Average continues going straight down, and now he finds it difficult to sit in his easy chair when the news is on and he tends to pace up and down. Finally, he decides, "if it drops below the 800 level, I don't care what my broker says, I'm getting out."

That evening on the TV news it is announced that the Dow Jones Industrial Average broke through the 800 level in the "worst single daily loss since President Kennedy's assassination." Experts are baffled since "the economic picture is favorable and the unemployment rate is the lowest in four years." That does it. The next morning as the market opens, a broker's phone is ringing and Mr. GrimJaw "bails out."

This drama is enacted usually two or three times per year; again it is the mass psychological approach of which the Dow Jones Industrial Average is the governing *trigger*. Thus there is a definite psychological impact to the Dow Jones Industrial Average that must be reckoned with, not only as it applies to others, but as it applies to ourselves. Even the best investors seldom escape this emotional influence of a falling Dow Jones Industrial Average.

Part II

THE BLUEPRINTS

"If you want to succeed you should strike out on new paths rather than travel the worn paths of accepted success."

JOHN D. ROCKEFELLER

STOCK MARKET BLUEPRINTS

In the following pages it will be my purpose to lay down specific plans of investment action based on the factors discussed in Part I of this book. No attempt has been made to explore every possible course of action open to the investor, but specifically those which in the opinion of the author attempt at all times to *maximize* the probabilities of success. Critics may say that these blueprints do not adequately allow for differences of opinion or methods of approach that could be applied by investors. No attempt has been made to allow for a difference of opinion in these pages. One should begin his investment thinking by recognizing that in order to be successful year after year a PLAN is of the utmost necessity. First he must determine what factors are most likely to lead to the success of that plan. Then the remaining steps are selection of the goal desired in a specific time period, and finally, the selection and subsequent purchase of those issues which meet with as many prerequisites to success as possible.

Now all this may sound ever so easy or logical to those who have never invested, but strangely enough, few investors can describe their plan other than to say they desire to make money.

I have discussed in an earlier chapter those factors which are most likely to lead to success. Now it becomes necessary to select the desired goal of your investment plan. Below are the four basic investment goals, along with the approximate time required to accomplish each.

The *blueprints* that follow are no more than an attempt to find the right type of stock to accomplish the desired goal. While not always the case, it should be assumed that the greater the percentage appreciation desired, and the shorter the span of time, the greater the risk involved. It is also generally true that the faster the rate of climb desired, the greater the day to day volatility is likely to be.

Thus, in the selection of a realistic blueprint to follow for the next decade, careful consideration should be given both to

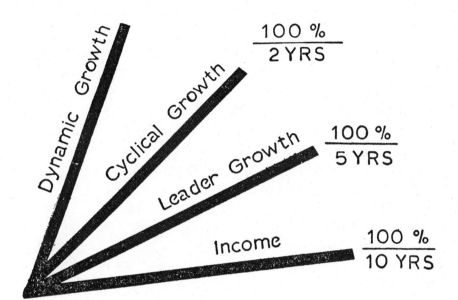

$$\frac{500\ \%}{2\ YRS}$$

$$\frac{100\ \%}{2\ YRS}$$

$$\frac{100\ \%}{5\ YRS}$$

$$\frac{100\ \%}{10\ YRS}$$

Dynamic Growth

Cyclical Growth

Leader Growth

Income

the degree of risk that must be assumed and the investor's own emotional temperament. For example, investors choosing the "income" or "leader growth" plans will usually spend much less time in watching and managing their portfolios than those in the "cyclical growth" and "dynamic growth" categories. The reason should be obvious: stocks likely to appreciate only 100% in ten years, or an average of 10% per year, are not going to be displaying any fireworks in the price action department. During a one year period, an investor desirous of definite market price action would go "wild" sitting around waiting for this type of issue to come to life. They seldom do more than creep along and, typically, move very much in line with the general market movement, though they are seldom as volatile. These same conclusions are very apt to be true of the leader growth issues also. But they should be definitely moving somewhat faster than the income issues.

The leader growth plan is for investors who like to have their funds invested in "big name" companies in different fields. There is no questioning the fact that some investors "feel" comfortable in stocks like Coca Cola or Sears, but may lose sleep or become very nervous holding a stock like Royal Crown Cola.

Other investors will want to have definite "action" most all of the time. Up or down, they want to see some activity. These investors will naturally select stocks likely to have this type of action within a year or so.

The cyclical growth plan selects from relatively high quality stocks, choosing those whose characteristics are definitely cyclical. This fact implies from the very beginning the necessity for a definite sale at the end of the cyclical swing. Such action may not be the case with leader growth or income plans.

Finally, the dynamic growth plan shoots at very high goals of appreciation in a short span of time. In most cases, these will be relatively new companies, or companies with new products or services, which may prove to be the outstanding blue chips of the future. They are surrounded by many unknown or unproven factors.

Basically, these plans are no more than the difference between people. Certainly if all investors had the time and desire and, yes, the emotional fortitude, they might select the dynamic growth blueprint. But the facts of investment life are very clear on this point. All investors do not have the same goals or objectives in mind, and many investors are quite content with a slower rate of change with less risk and higher quality.

One thing I am totally against, and that is the theory that a person's *age* is some criterion for selection of an investment blueprint. I have read some well-known columnists for years who pass out the advice that because one is a widow and 65 years of age she "should invest in nothing but solid blue chip issues paying the highest dividend return." Nothing, in my opinion, can be more misleading than this blanket approach to nice little old ladies, or for that matter, the similar approach that says, "The young executive should invest in nothing but growth issues." I have seen many elderly ladies who were pros in the management of their investment funds and could accept greater risks because they simply had more experience, as well as the time and desire to dig out the facts. And many young executives would be far better off sticking with a less dynamic plan even though it is slower, simply because they are too busy as executives to *properly* investigate the more volatile areas.

Thus a plan must be tailored to the desires and needs of each individual investor, and for any person or book to tell you precisely what plan is best for you would be foolhardy. What this book is attempting to do is to explore the four basic plans in depth, so that investors may have a clear idea of what choice is available to them and how to decide which plan, or combination of plans, best fits their individual requirements.

Each of these plans requires the step-by-step approach outlined in previous chapters in order to insure success.

Chapter VIII

THE INCOME BLUEPRINT

The income blueprint seeks the issue within an uptrend group that is paying the highest dividend return. The income plan is a very simple and long range plan. The basic desire of the investor is safety of principal and above average dividend return. These two factors must be considered as one, as it will be remembered in our discussion of types of stocks that a recessive stock will many times offer an exceptional yield. So the very first step of this plan is to be sure that the earnings of any company under consideration are in a gradually rising phase. A past period of no less than ten years should be considered. As all investment concerns itself with the future—not the past— the questions to be answered are: "Is this industry likely to grow in the years ahead" and "Is the stock under consideration likely to be a participant in that growth?"

These questions are certain to take more thought than you may at first believe, because of your inherent emotions that accept things as they are *today* and fail to consider what they will be like ten years hence. Few people can see beyond tomorrow. Successful income investors must be looking years ahead. A classic example is the demise of the importance of the railroads as a primary means of transportation and the rise of the airlines. Turn your mental clock back to the 1920's and early 1930's. At that time, the railroads were in their prime and the upstart airlines were a novelty, almost a joke. As an investor of that period, it was hard to arrive at a conclusion that the railroads would eventually become a secondary means of transportation for both passengers and possibly even cargo. The average investor was swept along with the concept of solidarity of rail issues, their asset value, their record of dividend payment, their blue chip aspects. These were factors few investment men could argue against; but as future facts proved, the rails were past their prime of life and during the next 30 years showed a steady decline. Yes, there were periods of time when the rail issues went up, and yes, there were always exceptions. But an investor desiring the income plan is forced to consider very long trends and then make the decision as to whether the industry in question is likely to continue to grow or not. Remember, no matter how big the dividend, it won't make up for a loss in principal.

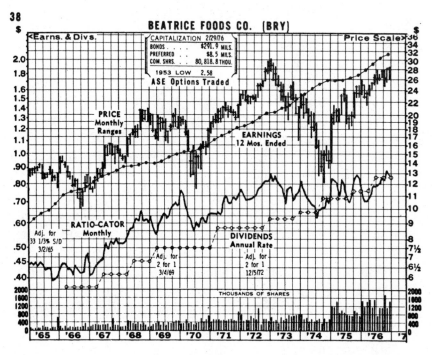

CYCLI-GRAPH chart by Securities Research Company, a Division of United Business Service Co., 208 Newbury St., Boston, Mass. 02116

Before leaving this thought of projecting yourself ahead, let us examine a current example. The automobile industry has just completed three record-breaking years of sales, and the World War II population boom is beginning to bring in more and more prospective buyers in the immediate years ahead. Also, a high percentage of families today have two cars or more. The automobile has become an indispensable necessity of life. I seriously doubt that I could get much of an argument on this fact at the men's club or even among a group of astute investors. *But*, let's look ahead. Is the automobile here to stay?

At this moment in history does this sound a little ridiculous? You bet it does—*today.*

Let's examine a few factors: the period following World War II saw the emergence of air travel to the point where even some grandmothers, who a generation ago swore they would never fly, are today hopping around the world without the slightest hesitation. We are, as these words are being written, engaged in a "limited" war in Southeast Asia, in which helicopters are playing an ever-increasing role. For over 20 years now, various companies have been working on the development of a small, vertical takeoff aircraft which would someday find a vast personal and commercial market. How many years it will be until some firm develops such an aircraft is hard to say, but the important thing is that it is a distinct possibility, maybe not too many years from now.

Now, returning to the question, "Is the automobile here to stay?", certainly it is. But the real question is: is it likely to play a more increasing role in our lives or are there means of personal transportation now on the drawing boards that will diminish the importance of automobiles in our society? I believe that a rational investor would have to concede, from the evidence now available, that automobiles are likely to play a diminishing role in the years ahead.

This example will, I hope, help you to gain a perspective in the search for industries that are very likely to have a steady upward slope to their earnings. For many years the solution, when seeking safety and gradual appreciation, has been to invest in those industries whose profits are gained by population growth. The prime example in recent years has been utilities. Others might include foods, food chains, banks and life insurance companies. Like all industries these will run hot and cold from time to time but in most instances their earnings rise steadily as population expands.

This, then, will give us some clue to the type of stocks we will be choosing in order to satisfy this basic plan. Our key thought is *stability of earnings* and a gradual upward trend in price. This is the major selection consideration. Half to two-thirds of our plan is already beginning to work by the simple elimination from our consideration of those issues that display wild earnings' gyrations or downward trends, or those issues that do not have adequate dividend yields to satisfy our basic objective of receiving better than average return. Three-quarters of the job of investment is the selection of the proper vehicle that is *even likely* to accomplish the desired goal. This is really not so difficult if one starts from the beginning with a clear idea of what one is looking for.

The other part of the task is to make our purchase at approximately such a time as to secure, hopefully, little or no downside risk plus the largest yield. To accomplish this feat requires a clear understanding that there will be on an average only ten to twelve ideal general market buy points in our investment career. Because the issue that we are seeking has only a gradual upward trend in earnings, it will tend to be swept along with the general tide of mass market movements, particularly at the extreme phases (bottoms or tops). Thus, we find our income type of stock typically on the bargain counter and also displaying exceptional yield at the general market bottoms.

Gauging what is a better than average yield at any given time is best accomplished by determining what the average yield is for some list of high grade issues. Again, the guide that has been most widely used for years is the Dow Jones Industrial Average. Thus, if the Dow Jones Industrial Average yield is 4%, then a better than average yield would be 5% to 6%. If the average is 3%, then 4% to 5% would again be better than the average.

The plan must also weigh the possibility of leaving one's money in the bank, should interest rates be almost equivalent to current dividend returns. A rough rule of thumb may be that unless one can secure a *minimum* of 50% more than the bank interest, then serious consideration should be given to leaving the money in the bank.

Theoretically, the *ideal* purchase time for an income type issue would be as follows:

1. The general market has been falling for several months and now levels off.
2. The earnings for the issue selected have continued upward and have a history of only minor variation.
3. The issue selected is selling near its historically low P/E ratio.
4. The dividend return is 50% higher than the Dow Jones Industrial Average group yield and 50% or more better than bank interest rates.

As these ideal conditions only exist an average of three times in each ten year period, it takes patience and courage to put this plan into action. When one stresses safety as a primary concern, it must be clearly remembered that after a general market decline, and after an individual issue has declined for some time, the risk of continued decline becomes lower and lower. Getting or seeking the absolute bottom is foolhardy as only sheer luck will make it possible.

Buying quality issues at depressed prices, with yields better than that of the average dividend return, should accomplish this goal of 100% appreciation in a ten year period and make for many restful nights of sleep.

Chapter IX

THE LEADER GROWTH BLUEPRINT

The leader growth plan seeks as its basic goals, first companies that are dominant or clearly leaders in their respective industries, and secondly, ones that have a proven record of increasing earnings and showing only minor variations in a rate of growth approximately 15% to 25% per year.

If the first two conditions above can be met, then generally a traditionally high-low P/E multiple can also be determined. On Page 134 is a chart which is representative of stocks with these basic factors. Note how consistent the trend for the earnings of this giant world-wide company has been.

Both private and institutional investors show a great preference for this type of issue and therefore, these issues are seldom on the bargain counter except after major market declines. Because this fact is so often true, timing the purchase of such stocks is, as it was the case in the income plan, closely associated with the major market indicator approach discussed in Chapter II (on indicators). This is an important fact to recognize for it makes a day to day check of these issues unnecessary when considering purchase. It is also important that the issues be purchased at their traditionally low P/E valuation in order to accomplish the objective of 100% appreciation in five years.

I believe this is probably the most satisfactory plan for beginning investors or those who cannot devote much time to the management of their funds. It is satisfactory primarily because it will produce good results if the plan is followed, and at all times there is the peace of mind inherent in the quality and the size of companies selected.

Knowing only what previous earnings have been can be dangerous when attempting to project future earnings, but, strangely enough, certain companies have had such outstanding records in their "rate of change" improvement, that their projected earnings have proven to be almost precisely on target. Of primary importance, when in the final selection process, is to determine from the best analytical sources if any change in this rate of earnings growth factor is "anticipated." This is not always easy to determine, but sometimes may be detected from the quarter to quarter figures, or from special reports or speeches given by company management.

Below is a list of stocks that, during the past ten years, have displayed some of the most consistent and best rate of earnings growth in their respective industries:

Air Products
American Hospital Supply
American Home Products
American Natural Resources
AMP, Inc.
Avon Products
Beneficial Corp.
Borden Co.
Bristol Myers
Central & Southwest Corp.
Citicorp
Coca Cola
Crown Cork & Seal
Disney (Walt)
Dr. Pepper
Digital Equipment
Eastman Kodak

Eckerd (Jack)
Emerson Electric
General Mills
Goodyear Tire & Rubber
Gulf & Western Industries
Halliburten
Hewlett-Packard
International Business Mach.
International Tel. & Tel.
Johnson & Johnson
Kresge
Louisiana Land &
   Exploration
Marriott
Masco
McDonald's
Melville Corp.

Merck & Co.	Schlumberger
Minnesota Mining & Mfg.	Sears, Roebuck
Nalco Chemical	Standard Brands
Perkins Elmer	Texaco, Inc.
Petrie Stores	Texas Eastern Corp.
Proctor & Gamble	Winn-Dixie Stores
Reynolds (R. J.) Industries	Xerox

Since the earnings trend for these issues has been extremely consistent over the past decade or longer, the most important variables have been the general market, group trend, and the P/E multiple.

Thus, as this plan is put into action, we start by noting that the general market as measured by the Dow Jones Industrial Average has dropped 10% to 30% or more and the indicators are beginning to suggest a "major bottom" is near. In a review of the industry groups it will be found that a few groups are in relative strength uptrends, not because the price of their stocks has been advancing strongly, but because they have been dropping less. This is one of the outstanding clues as to where the early investment demand is likely to be when the down pressure subsides and a new uptrend gets underway.

Next a review of the groups to determine the issue that best qualifies as the "quality leader" should be made. Now the probabilities are extremely high that the issue selected as the quality leader will also be in a relative strength *uptrend*. If so, the next step is to move on to the fundamental study of earnings and the P/E ratio levels. Should this stock not be in a relative strength uptrend, but be neutral or down, a "no buy, but watch for signs of life" policy should be followed. Assuming a clear relative strength uptrend, and earnings projections indicate continued upward trend in earnings, and current stock price is close to traditionally low P/E valuation, then a definite action to buy some should follow. The total amount purchased at this point depends considerably upon your total portfolio picture, but as a

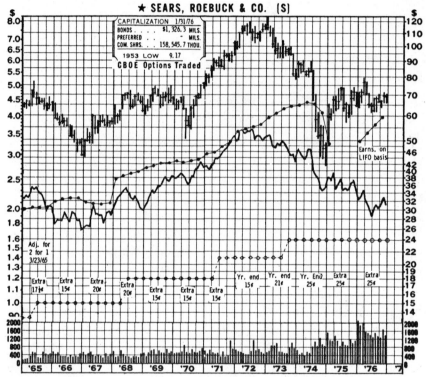

★ SEARS, ROEBUCK & CO. (S)

CAPITALIZATION 1/31/76
BONDS . . . . $1,326.3 MILS.
PREFERRED . . . - MILS.
COM. SHRS. . . 158,545.7 THOU.
1953 LOW 9.17
CBOE Options Traded

Earns. on LIFO basis

Adj. for 2 for 1 3/23/65

Extra 17¢ Extra 15¢ Extra 20¢ Extra 20¢ Extra 15¢ Extra 15¢ Extra 15¢ Yr. end 15¢ Yr. end 21¢ Yr. End 25¢ Extra 25¢ Extra 25¢

CYCLI-GRAPH chart by Securities Research Company, a Division of United Business Service Co.,
208 Newbury St., Boston, Mass. 02116

rough guide, buy approximately one-third of the estimated total position desired. Make the additional purchase only after a *profit* in the first commitment has been achieved, and as definite upward price action confirms your earlier conclusions regarding relative strength.

The reason for this "put-your-toe-in" approach is twofold. First, no one knows the exact bottom of the general market downswing, and what may appear as a bottom may within a few weeks have proved to be only a lull in the downswing. Thus, acquire only one-third of the desired position and then place a stop loss order approximately 10% below the purchase price. This will keep your losses minimal.

Secondly, occasionally certain stocks may not come down during the general market break, thereby giving the appearance of good relative strength, but when the trend turns back up, they fail to rise. While this phenomenon does not happen often, it does frequently enough to follow the prescribed policy of accumulating the additional two-thirds position *only* after a definite profit of 10% to 20% has been established in the original purchase.

This plan requires that the entire position desired is purchased approximately no more than 30% off the bottom prices for the stock and approximately 30% above the traditionally low P/E valuation.

In actual practice, your survey of the industry groups has led to the selection of five to ten different industries in definite relative strength uptrends. Having done the necessary homework, your decision is to place funds in several different stocks in approximately the same time period. Certainly not necessarily the same day—for remember, at bottoms, there is *no rush* to buy. So what if you do miss the absolute bottom price; you will reap many dollar rewards if you pay a little more when your indicators are continuing to say "buy" and if, *in fact*, stocks are beginning to *slowly* move higher.

Let us assume a $100,000 portfolio in cash all nicely await-ing a major bottom. This idea of being 100% in cash at the bottom is, I admit, rather ideal and would obviously allow for some objective appraisal of the situation, not having received many bloody scars from the previous crash. However, here lies a tremendous advantage that many private investors have—which the average institutional investor does not have—and that is the ability to return to a total cash (or the equivalent) posi-tion in order to ride out the major downswing. Large institu-tional investors — such as banks, insurance companies, mutual funds, etc.—have such large holdings of individual issues that when prices begin to fall they cannot truly "sell out," because the very fact that they were sellers would help depress prices further. Any such action on their part would be self-defeating. Believe me, the ability to be "always liquid," meaning the ability to sell your position out completely tomorrow without phasing the market price more than a fraction of a point or so, is one of the very big plus factors enjoyed, but seldom recognized or taken advantage of by private investors. Many big fund mana-gers would love to have the same liquidity, but are forced to ride the dips through by shifting only a portion of their funds into cash, notes, or bonds and hoping their remaining common stock portfolio will prove "defensive."

As we begin to invest this $100,000, the first step is to employ approximately one-third of the total amount, or $33,000. At this major bottom it should be possible to select at least five groups in definite uptrends, thus $33,000 should be invested in equal dollar amounts in these five industries.

The bottom or starting portfolio may look something as follows:

STARTING PORTFOLIO

Total: $100,000.
Amount to be invested now: $33,000.
Approximate number of industries selected: five.

Best five groups selected:

		Total Value
1.	Autos: 130 shrs. General Motors at $50	$6,500.
2.	Drugs: 100 shrs. Bristol-Myers at $70	7,000.
3.	Oils: 80 shrs. Texaco at $80	6,400.
4.	Soft Drinks: 60 shrs. Coca Cola at $110	6,600.
5.	Paper: 200 shrs. Scott Paper at $30	6,000.

$32,500.

Notice the disregard for "round lots," but more precisely buying dollar amounts. After all, our task is not to become collectors of stock certificates, but managers of money. The last step before final purchase is to make a clear decision as to where the stop loss should be placed, actual or mental, below the purchase price. I recommend these stop losses be placed no more than 10% below the purchase price, but this should be adjusted to slightly below a low of the trading range or any panic lows which may have developed.

After these purchases have been made, there is not much more to do except to wait and see if your judgment has been correct.

Now that you own these issues, a very strange phenomenon begins to come over the average investor, that is, an emotional response begins to occur as prices begin to fall toward the stop loss point: fear sends a chill up the spinal cord, or possibly a grin of joy appears when the first selection moves upward with a burst to establish a 10% profit. Make no mistake, you are wired in on the emotional circuit and your purely objective appraisal of these situations is likely to be tarnished.

In any case, major market bottoms occur so infrequently that this is not the time to go on a world cruise. A cursory appraisal of your purchases at least once each week, and with a watchful eye on other areas that appear attractive but where the trend was not so positive, is sufficient.

Approximately 45 calendar days past the time of the first purchase, a total review of all industry groups should be made. This is done first, to insure that the industries and issues already selected are continuing to do well, and also in order to watch for the emergence of new group strength. Assuming that two of the stocks already purchased show profits of approximately 10%, two show losses of approximately 10%, and one is about even, then what action should be taken? First try to avoid the big temptation of "cashing in" on the profits and continuing to hold the losses. This is the big downfall of most investors. In actuality, the plan is to acquire more of those issues that are definitely showing the strongest trend in price. Thus, another $6,000 worth of those issues that have a profit should be purchased at the advanced price levels. Stop losses are still in force, protecting those issues which have not moved higher. No additional action should be taken with these issues. Should another group and stock appear attractive, then purchase approximately $6,500 worth of this new stock.

In these early days of the new uptrend, it may be desirable to have more industry groups represented, but I strongly advise no more than ten for a $100,000 portfolio. (A few less for smaller sums and a few more for larger portfolios.) More than ten groups becomes very difficult to manage for it requires just that many more decisions. The average investor will postpone a decision, particularly if there "isn't enough money in the position to worry about." This type of thinking can be ruinous to a potentially good investor as it usually leads to making "no decisions" when decisions are necessary to preserve possible profits or to avoid losses. This leads to another market truism: "Buy enough to make it worthwhile or don't buy any." If 20% of your funds are concentrated in a stock which suffers some major reversals, you are likely to make a positive decision at the first sign of trouble, thereby holding your loss to a small percentage. There is no disgrace in the stock market in beating a hasty retreat in order to "live to fight another day." Too often, however, if you own only a small amount of a stock, a decision to sell is rationalized by the statement, "I don't own enough to get hurt."

Approximately 90 days past the date of the original purchase, another complete market, industry, stock and portfolio survey should be made. If the indicators remain favorable, and *in fact* your portfolio is continuing to steadily improve, then more decisions should be made and action taken. Do not expect to get any reassurance by reading about the economy. Most of the economic news will be bad and the stock market is a cold topic of discussion. Your biggest strength and encouragement is that you have not been completely stopped out of your original purchases and, as a matter of fact, most of them by now should be showing some profits. Look carefully at *what* is happening. Time after time I have seen people get talked out of very excellent positions because of some emotional friends or associates who have hit the panic button and bailed out right on the bottom. Thus having become totally convinced that the market was heading lower, they attempt to talk you into selling "while the rally lasts."

Counter each bearish discussion with the thought that the majority of people are usually wrong at the bottom. Be prepared for "bears" and stick to the facts of your own portfolio.

Assume that after 90 days you are continuing to show profits in the groups you bought more of after the 45 day review. The odds highly favor that these positions will turn out extremely satisfactorily over the next year or two, and already the bulk of funds are in these groups, so buy another $6,500 worth of these issues at the advanced prices. If you have been stopped out of any of the other positions, then there is no decision except the reemployment of the funds generated by the sale.

If, on the other hand, you have not been stopped out, but the issue hasn't moved up in price within the 90 days from purchase, a definite shift to another area is recommended. By now more groups should begin to show good strength, as the new general market advance broadens. The problem of selection becomes more difficult because there are more candidates that qualify. Shift dormant funds to new areas of strength and continue to pursue the policy of close stop losses from the purchase price.

You now have two *full* positions that appear solid for the long term and you are searching for three more. This process continues to repeat itself, that is, eliminating the weak or dormant ones and adding funds to the strong ones until five *full* 20% (approximately) positions have been established.

Once these five positions are established and each should have at least 25% profit from the first purchase price (not necessarily the last price paid), you have accomplished the first part of the investment blueprint, which is to become *fully invested within three to six months past a major bottom.*

What's next? Nothing . . . relax and enjoy it.

Now that you are fully invested there is not really much to do for the next few months but to make sure that none of your selections breaks its upward trend in price or relative strength. There will be some more dynamic issues going up at a faster rate than yours and the temptation is always to say, "I should have bought Xerox" or some other high flyer. But according to this plan, you have eliminated many of these high flyers simply because you desire proven quality and leadership. Many of the high flyers of today may eventually qualify in your selection process, maybe at the next major bottom, but not today.

The stocks you have selected should move along steadily showing definite progress month by month, but the day-to-day action will not be thrilling. This, in fact, is the time to take that world cruise. To date we have never had a major market move that lasted less than 12 months from bottom to top. (When we do, it will probably signal a period of extreme weakness ahead. So should you be on a cruise and you learn that the market has suddenly grown weak—come home fast.)

Having established a long term (nine months to a year) profit in each of the five groups, the next step is to look for some indications of a top for these issues, not necessarily for the general market. Remember that as the general market advances, early group leaders sometimes give way to other groups that are late starters. One of the best *keys* for the selling of these early quality leaders has been their traditionally high P/E ratios. Thus, if Texaco, who in recent years has had a high P/E ratio of 21 times earnings, is currently selling in that area, and projected earnings indicate no unusual change in the rate of growth for these earnings, then a definite decision must be arrived at:

1. to sell: thus establishing a profit on which capital gains tax would apply.
2. to hold: recognizing a dormant sideways trend or a downtrend in price is likely to follow.

These are the only two choices open to investors when they believe that a top has been reached. There is a great deal of confusion on this point as there are also long-long term investors in the market who will follow what is called the "lock box philosophy," that is, buying high grade securities and putting them away for ten to 20 years. This philosophy has proved successful for some investors during the past 30 years or so and, if investors desire this approach, the blueprints of income and leader growth are the best suited. However, the lock box philosophy requires that investors continue to hold stocks, when in fact the probabilities of success over a several years period are against them. Their "hope" is that the quality and size of the company's issues selected preclude a "major loss."

Few investors today realize that it was 1958 before the bluest of the blue chips—American Telephone—was able to better its 1929 high point. For these reasons, and because at all times the blueprints in this book attempt to maximize the probability of success, the recommended policy of this plan is to sell these leader growth issues as they hit in the vicinity of their traditionally high P/E ratios, thus avoiding the sideways or downward trend.

This is best accomplished by placing a 10% stop loss behind the stock as it approaches this area; place the stop at 5% if it hits the traditional level and keep it moving 5% or less behind the price on any movement above the traditionally high P/E level. Many times these issues will take a "spurt" up above the traditional P/E area but it seldom lasts long. What is likely to change the accuracy of this type of approach is simply a significant change in the earnings growth rate, and while this is unlikely, it is possible.

Another reason, and possibly a more important one than the above two, for selling these issues is that, at the top, no one knows how far down is the bottom, which may not occur for several years.

The only remaining question then is, "How about the taxes?" No one likes to pay taxes, but once beyond the six month holding period to qualify for the long term capital gains tax, there is no further tax advantage possible, unless you plan to die in order to leave it to your heirs. This latter point is not an investment decision. As our tax laws change, so will the character of stock price movement, but under the existing laws there is absolutely no tax advantage to holding a stock beyond nine-months to a year. Thus, the only valid reason for holding a stock beyond the tax period is the investment decision that the price is going higher. If you think that the price is going lower, then there can't be any rationalization or justification for continued holding. Sell!

While the concept of traditionally high P/E valuations is the best method I have discovered as a selling guide to the leader growth issues, other determinants of topping action must be kept in mind, e.g., break of a major trendline, unusual percentage dip, or group trend breakdown. Assume approximately one year past the major market bottom that one of the five issues selected reaches its traditionally high P/E valuation, but the others have still further to go. As a sale is advised, the cash generated must be re-employed or placed in the bank to receive the interest. Before re-investment, a general market review should be made to determine the approximate strength or weakness of the major market. If indicators suggest a mid-point or slightly beyond, then re-investment in a new emerging group having the same or similar qualifications as the original purchase should be made. Again, follow the procedure of dividing the funds into thirds and this time phasing into one to three new stocks, utilizing stop loss orders below the purchase price and again buying more of the strong ones, while eliminating or reducing the dormant or weak ones.

About two years past the major bottom, most of the economic factors will again be quite bright. Many of your friends and business associates have returned to the market, and because stocks have been generally rising for two years, many now have some profits which fuel their enthusiasm. By now, however, you have noted that several of your original purchases are approaching their traditionally high P/E valuations and in fact you have established some very good profits during the past two years ranging from about 75% to 125%. A check of the general market indicators suggests a top is approaching. Should an outstanding quality issue be just turning up, a reduced position in this stock may be purchased, but the major policy is to begin to raise cash and to await a better buying opportunity.

Your reasoning here is that while some individual groups and issues will still continue strong, the advent of general market weakness is likely to slow their upward progress or reverse it to the downside. The recognition of impending weakness is possible but the extent or magnitude of the decline is not. Thus, while a policy of raising cash in the final stages of the up move can be for the moment very frustrating (as some issues are literally flying up 5% to 10% a day), it assures profits and allows for objective thinking at the next major bottom.

As the first stage of the market downswing gets underway, no more than a 50% invested position should remain and that should be only in the leading market groups. All stocks with a sideways or downward relative strength trend should be immediately eliminated if this has not already been accomplished. The leading relative strength stocks are typically, at this stage, the last to fall and thus may make new highs even as the market downswing continues. Eventually, however, as the market downswing accelerates, these stocks will also usually succumb to the down pressure, so that keeping stop loss orders on all remaining issues is advised.

By the time the next bottom is reached, a return to almost 100% cash probably will have occurred. Downswings come fast and give the investor few opportunities to correct any earlier errors. Giving up some profit on the top is a small "loss" compared to trying to "break even" in a bear market. Maintaining one's objectivity is difficult if one has just lost one's shirt.

Chapter X

THE CYCLICAL GROWTH BLUEPRINT

The cyclical growth plan again shoots at a greater amount of appreciation in a shorter time span, and differs essentially from the previous plan in that it selects stocks which historically have widely fluctuating earnings patterns.

While in the first two plans, the concept of steadily increasing earnings and relatively stable price moves over a five to ten year span is of prime importance, the cyclical growth plan seeks stocks of well-known companies whose earnings fluctuate sharply for relatively short periods of time, one to three years. During the rising phase the earnings typically have all the appearance of dynamic growth issues, but historically have not been able to continue at such sharply rising rates. In most cases, these companies are in mature, highly competitive fields, where general economic conditions have a great influence on their profitability. Knowing which industries are typically cyclical is important. (Review Chapter V.)

The cyclical growth plan seeks a minimum goal of 100% appreciation in approximately a two-year span. Many times, 200% to 300% may be attainable, but, as may be expected when shooting for these higher rewards, the investor must also expect to find the job more difficult and requiring more time, study and decisions.

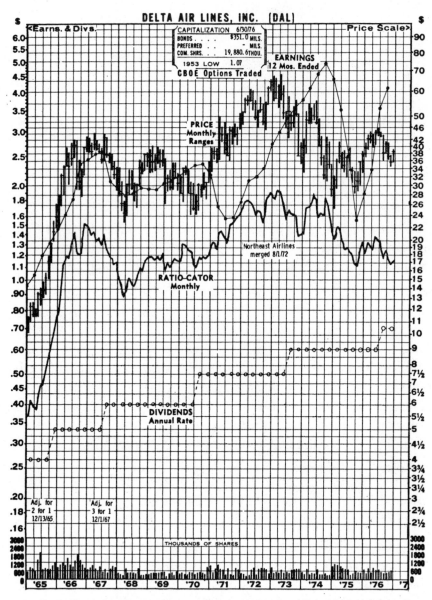

DELTA AIR LINES, INC. (DAL)

The problems with this plan are listed briefly below:

1. Requires great emotional control.
2. Investors must take action with greater reliance on technical evaluations rather than fundamental ones.
3. Because of a high degree of volatility, decisions and action must take place faster.
4. Requires buying when earnings are falling.
5. Requires buying when news is bad.
6. Requires buying after dividend omission or reduction.
7. Requires buying at high P/E ratios.
8. Requires selling when earnings are the best and rising.
9. Requires selling when news and reports are extremely good.
10. Requires selling after dividends have been raised.
11. Requires selling at low P/E ratios.
12. Requires the definite action of selling at the top of the swing, regardless of "quality," and is never to be considered a "lock box" candidate.

Now if the investor can stomach all of the above prerequisites, then the cyclical growth plan can be exciting and profitable.

A knowledge of the previous cycles is important to determine if the stock has traditionally had a mild cycle or a wild one. Generally speaking, the company with more borrowed funds in its total capitalization will *tend* to be more widely fluctuating. As an example, at the bottom of a cyclical swing, Company A on every $100 worth of sales has fixed costs of $20 and variable costs (those that vary primarily with production) of $60, leaving earnings of approximately $20 per $100 of sales. Company B has higher fixed costs of $35 per $100 of sales and variable costs of approximately $60, leaving only $5 earnings or profits on $100 worth of sales. Assume for illustrative pur-

poses that at the top of the swing both double their sales; the
figures would appear as below:

	Bottom of Cycle		Top of Cycle	
	Co. A	Co. B	Co. A	Co. B
Sales	$100	$100	$200	$200
Fixed Costs	20	35	20	35
Variable Costs	60	60	120	120
Profit	$ 20	$ 5	$ 60	$ 45

Company A is definitely the more efficient producer capable
of generating a higher profit margin on every dollar of sales.
But notice the relative percentage change in the profits in these
two examples. While Company A's profit has gone up 200%,
Company B's profit has gone up 800%. Thus, to the extent that
price anticipates the relative percentage change in earnings, we
would expect the price increase of Company B's stock to be
greater than that of Company A—certainly not necessarily the
exact same percentage change in earnings, but at least a substantial difference. Understanding that all stock price movement
is geared in some degree to the percentage change in profits, it
should be easier to understand why a stock having low or deficit
earnings shows greater change on the first sign of earnings improvement than a blue chip that shows a steady 10% increase
in its yearly profits. This point is extremely important to understand when seeking dynamic growth issues discussed in the next
chapter, but is also important when applied to cyclical issues.
Its importance to you as a prospective buyer of a cyclical stock
is that by simply looking at the current earnings figures during
the selection search, logic would almost demand that you select
Company A as the company operating more efficiently, whereas
Company B has a better chance of relative earnings improvement.

Secure a good long term chart book such as Securities Research *Cycli-graphs* and do a detailed study of the interworkings between earnings and prices. This will clearly reveal that

in 85% of the cases, the best time to have bought cyclical issues was when their earnings were falling sharply and their P/E ratios were relatively high. You might wonder how this can be reconciled with the previous blueprints and the earnings conclusions drawn from them. The answer is that it cannot be, because we are dealing with two entirely different breeds of cats. If you cannot shift conclusions to deal with an entirely different type of price movement then you should not attempt the cyclical growth plan, as it will not only confuse you but will cost you highly in terms of losses.

The *basic general market timing conclusions* as discussed in previous blueprints apply equally as you begin to invest in these cyclical issues. Now if the indicators suggest a market bottom, then your survey of groups and individual issues begins. Again, the primary focus tool is group relative strength, and now as earlier, an important comparative tool is the relative strength of the individual stocks. But, where, in previous plans, some yardstick of traditionally high-low P/E valuation was possible, such is not the case with cyclical issues. In previous plans, the rate of change in current and projected earnings was checked as a guideline before purchase. However, with cyclical issues the most important selection factor is that earnings are *falling*, which is not very reassuring. Thus, the single most important tool in the selection of cyclical stocks is relative strength for the group and individual stocks.

In other words, you must bet almost strictly on anticipation of better things to come because a look at current and recent past data will frighten off most investors. It becomes very important to understand that if the bad factors, as reported, are so bad, then why is this cyclical issue in a relative strength uptrend? The only answer is that big money is accumulating, under the guise of bad news, in anticipation of an improvement in the near future. This is certainly not much comfort to a prospective buyer, and it is why most investors are truly not suited for this type of issue. But following the relative strength trends for these issues allows for some handsome profits for those who clearly understand this inter-action. The question is often asked, "Why not wait until the earnings of these issues have clearly turned up before buying?" The answer is that by the time the earnings have clearly turned up, the stock is already a third to half way up the total swing, which generally increases the risk factor and at the same time reduces the potential. It can be done, and occasionally good profits are secured by shorter term traders. For the investor, however, buying in at a low risk bottom with full potential ahead is more desirable.

These cyclical issues, in order to reach their minimum objective of 100% appreciation in approximately two years, typically cannot sit still or move sideways much more than three or four months at a time before moving decisively higher. Hence these stocks are best suited for people who desire more definite action from week to week. If, however, a cyclical issue fails to continue its upward progress, after a four to six month period of sideways consolidation, a definite stop loss order placed under the lowest price in the current trading range is advisable. Often this four to six month sideways movement will turn out to be the top of the cyclical swing. Always be suspect of this factor.

Within a group, it is often possible to rotate from the early relative strength leaders to issues that have not yet shown as great a price appreciation. This type of action I call the "catch-up" concept. The reasoning behind such rotation within a group is relatively simple. The first early leader which in fact turns the group is usually the company that has been making the best steps forward to improve its profitability, but because of the general psychological depression towards its particular industry it has not shown any substantial price gains. As the most astute investors, research departments or even insiders dig into this company, they suddenly begin to realize that the efforts the company has been making to improve its profitability are about to pay off in terms of substantially improved earnings. Thus, regardless of the group's actions, they begin to buy this stock.

This very early leader is often the "crystal ball" that tells you the factors affecting this one stock may be improving for the entire group. No quality implication should be attached to the early leader however. The typical rotational order appears to be:

Non-Cyclical Groups:
1. Early leader.
2. Higher quality issues.
3. Secondary quality issues.
4. Speculative issues.

Cyclical Groups:
1. Early leader.
2. Speculative issues.
3. Secondary issues.
4. Quality leaders.

Here again we note the contrariness of the cyclical groups. The early leaders often appear as much as one year in advance of any concrete group activity. In any case, it should be recognized that the supply-demand factor must be balanced heavily in favor of excess demand when an individual stock is able to buck its current group trend. An example of this early leader concept occurred in early 1964 when Boeing turned into a solid uptrend, almost one year in advance of its group. Buying into Boeing even before its group turned up proved profitable, even though there proved to be 200% still to go after the group began to move higher.

However, Boeing's biggest competitor, Douglas, which was not in a clear uptrend for almost a year after Boeing made the turn, and had advanced only 50%, proved to be a better buy as a "catch-up" candidate by subsequently appreciating over 400%. Therefore, if you are an investor who doesn't like to buy into a stock after it has advanced 100% or more, then the concept of catch-up buying should prove satisfactory.

When dealing with cyclical groups it often becomes possible to buy into the higher quality issues *late* and at the same time secure some handsome yields and appreciation. This obviously is the "cake and eat it, too" philosophy, and like most things in the stock market, if you know where to look you have a better chance of finding the plum you are seeking.

As there are no traditional P/E ratios that have much meaning as a guide for selling these cyclical issues, different types of selling tools must be employed. A break of the upward trend-line is one of the best. Sideways moves for four to six months is another. Failure to make new highs when excellent earnings are reported is a third, and finally, too large a percentage dip is another. Finding the cyclical top is not easy, but if any one of the above factors occurs, then definite stop loss action is required. This is particularly true if the cycle has been up for longer than a year, very true at two years, and almost 100% true at three years. Remember, a stop loss order is designed to keep you *invested* in the stock, hopefully as long as there appears to be a chance that the trend will continue higher.

From time to time a whip-saw action will occur; this is why stop loss orders should not be placed unless the investor believes that a downside break would indicate a new downtrend beginning. It is far better to be sold out and be wrong than not to be sold out when the trend is headed lower. Never forget that downswings are much sharper and faster than the upswings.

The cyclical growth plan can be rewarding, not only because of handsome profits in a relatively short time, but also because in most cases the companies selected are large in size and assets and are among many of the basic industries. These latter factors give the investor a psychological feeling of safety, but make no mistake about falling in love with these issues. Few have been able to change their patterns, though the cycles may vary in length of time, and thus they are definitely candidates for sale at the top of the swing.

In the opening days of 1960, the longest steel strike on record came to an end. That day, U. S. Steel sold for a high of $69 a share. Two years later, at the low in 1962, the same stock sold for under $27. Four years later the stock was still selling under under $25 per share. His reason for buying in 1960 was that it was a blue chip and a respected leader in its field, and—after all—"steel" is the backbone of the nation. Today he is likely to mutter, "that dog." But big steel is not a dog; it is a cyclical company that has been steadily expanding its production capabilities and modernizing its methods. By the end of 1965, the company reported earnings of about $3.50 per share, yet the price of the stock was still one-half of its 1960 level. To one following a strictly fundamental approach, this is always a most perplexing point. He will argue at great length about the soundness, the assets, the quality and the outstanding value. I offer no argument except, *to whom?* Stocks are worth each day, week or year exactly what investors are willing to pay for them—no more and no less. Try to get a bank to make you a collateral loan on the basis that the stock once sold for $69 per share, or that you should receive a bigger percentage loan because the stock is "too cheap." The strict fundamentalist will further argue that some day investors will recognize these sound fundamental factors and the stock will move up again. Here I have no argument. But when is "someday"? In your investing lifetime or in your children's? If it takes too long, someone may find a better and cheaper material than steel, and then what?

Making a profit in cyclical issues demands extreme emotional control in order to be able to see through the "smoke" of good tidings and a "new era" at the top, and the blackness of doom and gloom at the bottom. Once mastered, however, cyclical issues can be very profitable.

Chapter XI

THE DYNAMIC GROWTH BLUEPRINT

This is the plan to get the big boomers or high flyers and the plan which many people hope to achieve, but seldom do. The reason for this lack of success is simply that most people have not taken the time to fully study the characteristics and behavior patterns of previous big winners. Should they get one of these boomers, it is mostly by luck and not by plan, and then in a high percentage of cases they cannot resist the temptation to "tie down" a 100% or 200% profit.

The first step to success in seeking the dynamic growth winners is to set a minimum goal for appreciation of 500% in approximately two years. This should immediately tell any investor with previous experience that we are truly looking for the needle in the hay stack.

It should further imply that the chances of success are limited and the *risks* involved are likely to be much greater than in the previous blueprints. Obviously, it is a plan suited primarily to certain types of investors: those who already have built up a sizable estate and those who are earning income in the highest brackets. In both cases, the ability to assume greater risks is required. This does not mean that investors following one of the other more conservative plans cannot place a portion of their investment funds in stocks which have "dynamic growth" potential, but if they do, they must learn the guidelines of this blueprint.

ECKERD (JACK) CORP. (ECK)

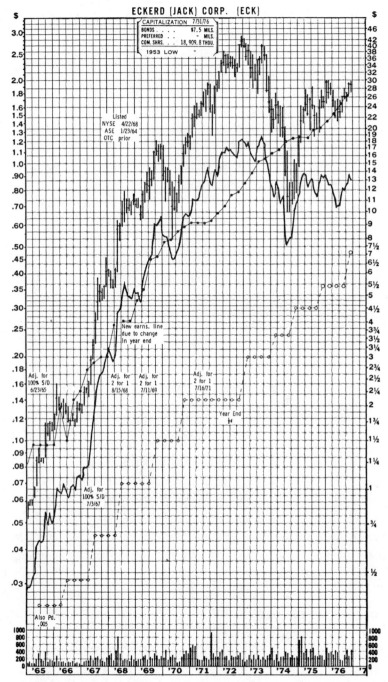

CAPITALIZATION 7/31/76
BONDS . . . . $7.5 MILS.
PREFERRED . . - MILS.
COM. SHRS. . . 18,909.8 THOU.
1953 LOW -

Listed
NYSE 4/22/68
ASE 1/23/64
OTC prior

New earns. line
due to change
in year end

Adj. for
100% S/D
6/23/65

Adj. for
2 for 1
8/15/68

Adj. for
2 for 1
7/11/69

Adj. for
2 for 1
7/16/71

Year End

Adj. for
100% S/D
7/3/67

Also Pd.
.005

'65 '66 '67 '68 '69 '70 '71 '72 '73 '74 '75 '76

CYCLI-GRAPH chart by Securities Research Company, a Division of United Business Service Co.,
208 Newbury St., Boston, Mass. 02116

By setting a minimum goal of 500% gain in two years, it should be obvious that the plan is searching for something new, different, or most unusual. This high goal immediately eliminates 98% of all issues. Ask yourself what possible factors could *change* companies such as General Motors, Bank of America, General Telephone, Standard Oil of California, or Safeway Stores to make their stocks rise by 500% in the next two years. The answer is that while it is not impossible, the likelihood is very remote. Thus, we automatically eliminate all such companies as even possible contenders and ask the question, "What conditions or factors are likely to allow for the kind of change that will accomplish our desired goal?"

The answer can be boiled down to approximately four major areas where dynamic change is even likely to occur. These are:

1. New companies.
2. New products or services.
3. Aggressive acquisition.
4. High leverage situations.

This narrows the field of search greatly.

New Companies

New issues are typically companies that have been in business a relatively short time and may or may not have some unusual products or services. Without something "special" in their product mix, you can expect these companies to sell relatively in line with their respective industry competition. Many times new issues will be first offered for public sale when the balance sheet looks its best, only to have some "unexpected difficulties" arise in the following year. In other cases, however, the companies may not fit into any group classification but may have a rather unique product or service. These stocks must be studied in much greater detail because, *if* they are successful, the relative change in the company in those early years can be extremely significant. It is far easier to double the sales of new products in demand than it is to double the sales of proven well-established ones. It is important that this point be clearly understood. There may be greater safety and reliability in the large companies with proven products, but there is likely to be greater *change* in the unproven small companies.

If we return to one of the basics in Chapter V, it is the rate of change in profits that is ultimately the most important factor in the rate of change in price. Thus relatively small companies with products or services in demand are capable of extremely rapid growth rates in their early years.

New Products or New Services

New ideas are not restricted to new companies. Haloid Corp. (later Xerox) had been in business for 26 years when it first took on the development of the xerography process, which later made the company's stock the outstanding dynamic growth issue for over a decade. On the other hand, RCA, which pioneered the development of color TV and at one point had almost a complete monopoly on color tubes, proved to be one of the worst performers, percentage-wise, in the color TV boom of the mid-1960s. The reason was that even with this monopoly on a new product, it only formed a small percentage of the total earning capacity for RCA. And while RCA did well, Admiral—whose earnings were more affected by the color TV boom—turned in a far superior performance.

Thus a new product or development must be placed in its proper perspective as to its total possible impact on the company which develops it. The biggest winner in the color TV boom was a little-heard-of, debt-ridden company with many years of poor earnings called National Video. National Video had worked for years to develop a rectangular color tube in direct competition to the giant RCA. As the demand for color sets suddenly began to grow and RCA could not supply the requirements of other manufacturers, National Video's big gamble paid off by several hundreds percent change in its earnings and the price of the stock easily made the minimum appreciation of 500% in a two-year period.

Aggressive Acquisition

Another area where dynamic change has occurred in the past, allowing a company to grow at an unusual rate, is by aggressive acquisition of other companies. One of the outstanding examples of this type of growth was Litton Industries, which, in approximately 14 years from its beginning grew into a company with $1 billion in sales, essentially through buying up companies and integrating them into one total operation. To the neophyte it may appear that this is the easy route for a company to *change* its value and, in turn, the price of its stock. If price were closely dependent on the assets of the concern this would be true. However, price is more closely related to profitability than to asset value, and it is no easy task to buy companies and at the same time keep them—or make them—profitable. It requires outstanding management skill in the selection, timing and integration of the new companies. One bad apple can ruin the whole pie for many years. It is a very real accomplishment when a company can grow by the acquisition route and still remain highly profitable. Litton's success was outstanding.

High Leverage Situations

Finally, the other major avenue that has allowed for sufficient change to accomplish a 500% price increase in two years has been by borrowing huge amounts of money. One of the more recent examples of this concept occurred in 1962 when a small paper and chemical company by the name of Albemarle Paper Company, which had sales of $14 million, offered to buy out Ethyl Gasoline Corp., a joint venture of Standard Oil of New Jersey and General Motors. It proposed to complete this transaction by borrowing $200 million from various banks and insurance companies. A Forbes Magazine article described this concept as "Jonah Swallowing the Whale."

The risks of such a venture are glaringly apparent. If successful, a relatively tiny company would become a giant almost overnight. If interest payments can be met, a significant change in the company's earnings is likely to occur. As the Ethyl story proved to be a smashing success, its stock went up over 1,000% in two years. If, however, the company had even barely stubbed its toe, it could also have been put in bankruptcy. The biggest assurance investors can have in such a situation is that the lenders of such huge sums of capital to a small firm are not likely to have made such a loan unless their investigations indicated a great probability of success.

These, then, are the four areas in the past which have allowed for a 500% gain in the price of a stock within a two-year period. The basic plan of attack is to look at these areas where significant change is occurring or is likely to occur. It does not require a 500% change in earnings in order to achieve a 500% gain in price. My studies have shown that approximately a 200% increase in earnings will generate approximately a 500% rise in price, provided that the earnings growth is likely to continue up, even at lesser rates of increase. This simply means the earnings are not cyclical nor likely to reverse after the initial burst. Hence, a stock which has appreciated 500% in a two-year period is not apt to be a candidate for another 500% appreciation in the following two years, unless it is again able to raise its earnings by 200% from the end of the second year to the end of the fourth year. This requires a growth rate of almost 100% per year in earnings, which becomes more and more difficult to achieve.

What is the best way to find these dynamic issues? Already we have explored where such growth is likely to be found. The first step is to become a very independent thinker, which is no easy task in these days of socialized everything. The next step is to become an avid reader, not only of the more standard investment news media such as Barron's, the Wall Street Journal, Forbes Magazine, Wall Street transcripts, etc., but also various trade magazines and journals. You are searching for ideas which, if proven successful, are likely to create an unusual demand in the immediate years ahead.

I have found certain ingredients or *keys* to be present among many of the dynamic growth issues of the past. Committing these keys to memory with a clear understanding of each should help in the recognition of a potential dynamic growth candidate.

KEYS TO DYNAMIC GROWTH STOCKS

KEY #1: *Big Gamble*

In most every case, a company with dynamic growth potential is one in which a *big gamble* was taken in the development of some new product or service. In most instances, the company was staking its life, so to speak, that the product or service would eventually prove highly profitable. If the product had failed, the company in all likelihood would be bankrupt. This is particularly true of a new or small company, and each year literally hundreds of companies whose big gamble failed do go bankrupt. What is important here is to understand that if you wanted to go into business for yourself you would also be taking on a big gamble and, if you had no partners or stockholders, you would also be taking on the "whole" gamble. However, as a prospective stock buyer in a company which is taking a big gamble, you will only share in the risk to the amount of your invested capital. Now the vast majority of new companies, and to a large degree those that will take on a big gamble project, will be companies in which the bulk of the stock is owned by management. This becomes another important key.

KEY #2: *Management Ownership*

It is always nice to know that the management of a company that assumes a big gamble situation has a big stake in the success or failure of the project. It must be assumed that logical, prudent management will do everything possible to make the company successful as they are likely to lose the most if it fails. Always check to determine how much of the big gamble company is directly owned by management. You may be amazed to find that management may own between 40% and 60% of the stock or more. Obviously, if the big gamble pays off, they stand to benefit the most; if it doesn't, they will lose the most. These are the facts of life which give you, as a prospective participant in the big gamble, some assurance that every effort will be made to make the project successful. A company where management has little stake in a big gamble project may in fact prove successful, but having management money in the pot also tends to keep everyone honest by eliminating many wild or hairbrained ideas.

KEY #3: *Farsightedness*

Companies who take on the big gamble project are in most cases looking a long way into the future. They recognize the fact that, if their project is successful, it may still require many years of development and promotion before any rewards will ever begin to occur. This requires a great deal of courage and tenacity on the part of the management, and a tremendous amount of patience on the part of the stockholders. The greatest mistake of even the most astute investor, who recognizes the full potential of the project, is to become impatient because the *price* of the stock fails to move as fast as he thinks it should. Thus, he sells out his positions far too early.

KEY #4: *Monopoly*

Look for companies whose products give them a virtual monopoly in the field, but not in the Justice Department sense of monopoly. As an example, the Polaroid camera did not have a monopoly in the photographic field, but they did have a specialized method of taking a picture and that particular method was a monopoly. Another example is Xerox: the xerography method of reproduction in the office copying field made them famous. Coca Cola might be considered in a similar light. What is extremely important to a company that has this type of monopoly is that it specializes and produces the highest quality products.

KEY #5: *Specialization*

Contrary to some widely held beliefs, diversification of products is not an asset for a dynamic growth company. The company which pioneers and develops new products or services should have no need for diversification in the early stages of its career. After all, the reason it is a dynamic growth company is because it has an insatiable *demand* for its products or services into the immediate years ahead. This requires undivided attention or specialization in order to supply that demand. Obviously, someday in the future—two, five, ten years hence—production may catch up with demand, thus requiring some diversification to keep the company growing.

The fact, however, that a company is looking for ways to diversify is the first sign that the demand for its products is beginning to ebb. Specialization does not necessarily imply only one product, but simply products closely aligned to one particular field.

KEY #6: *Quality*

While specialization is an essential key in the early stages of development, the quality of the products or services is an absolute essential for continued, year-after-year, success. This is true from two standpoints. First, the highest quality product will in the long run be the favorite among immediate users, irrespective of price. More often than not, the highest quality product is able to command and get a premium price, possibly 25%

to 50% above potential competition. This is true because consumers are always seeking the *best* product to accomplish their needs. Lesser quality products will wear out faster, require more repairs, and ultimately lead the consumer to pay the additional 25% to 50% more in order to secure the best. This is the root of the saying, "In the long run, the best is always the cheapest."

Secondly, from the company's standpoint, the production of the best quality products allows for a higher profit, without necessarily proportionately higher production costs. This means more earnings for the stockholders. It also means far fewer warranty repairs and, most important of all, it makes for satisfied users, who become the biggest "word of mouth" advertisers for future sales.

These three keys—monopoly, specialization, and quality—are among the most important of all those presented.

KEY #7: *Patents*

Patents are important to a new company with a new product, and having *good* patents and subsidiary patents is often the essential key to the monopoly discussed above. The essential feature, however, is how difficult it is for competition to enter the field and how fast they can be expected to do so.

Metrecal (liquid diet food) is an example of a company's pioneering a new concept in eating habits, but the company was only able to maintain its monopoly for a very short time. Competitors did not require any special equipment or know-how in order to compete.

Tight patents are not absolutely necessary for a dynamic growth company, but they are most welcome as an important key. The problem for the average investor, however, is to know just how strong the patents are. Unfortunately, the only answer is to watch for competition and to see if other companies are requesting patent license agreements. If so, then you can expect that patents are reasonably tight.

KEY #8: *Contrariness*

Watch for the company which bucks the prevailing trend. When the majority of autos are growing longer and longer, watch the company that enters the field with a small compact (for example, American Motors in 1958). Watch companies which break with tradition; they may start a new tradition.

This concept of contrariness is very important to a successful investor. It is much harder to think in terms of something new and different than it is to accept that which already exists. Most every major invention and development was, at the time of its inception, thought to be impractical, impossible, dangerous and of little or no future value. Successful investors can *never* think in these terms.

KEY #9: *Uncertainties*

Always surrounding new ideas, products or services are a multitude of uncertainties. By nature, the average investor likes to know all the facts or to "feel" that things are right. The "feel" concept is more of a familiarity with the company than any sound investment reasoning. With dynamic growth companies, however, he is very unlikely to *feel* confident. It is equally difficult to gain reassuring information since everyone from the president of the company to brokers recommending the stock will immediately concede that the situation is highly speculative with many problems and obstacles to hurdle before any profits can be obtained. Facts are always sparse and, more often than not, the information must be pieced together by clipping news announcements and obtaining company bulletins. These companies will rarely be mentioned in the leading investment services. Working with limited information, it is hardly likely that a person will "feel" much confidence, yet this is the typical situation where dynamic growth issues are concerned. This *key* of uncertainty occurs so often that a corollary may be "If it looks like a lead pipe cinch, look out."

KEY #10: *Check the Unbelievable*

Several times I have missed potentially outstanding situations because, when reading the information available, the ideas sounded preposterous or unbelievable. Months later, I watched the stock soar to unbelievable heights. Investors seeking big potential growth must develop a completely open and objective thought process. The unbelievable today may be fact tomorrow, so always check the unbelievable closely.

KEY #11: *Management*

Without doubt the most important key to a big gamble situation is management's ability to finally make the project successful. As mentioned in Key #2, it is nice to know that management has a stake in the venture. Equally important is to gain some insight into management's ability and philosophy. Appraising the ability of management is practically impossible for most investors except in hindsight. Did they succeed or fail? From time to time, however, it is possible to know their background. Sometimes managers will depart from one successful position to start their own company, as was the case with Tex Thornton of Litton Industries.

Even more important is to catch a glimpse of management's over-all philosophy. Are they truly looking far ahead? Are they exploring every avenue for their products? Is it their expressed purpose to make the company very large? Are the stockholders well advised or is it difficult to get information? Never forget the stockholders are the *owners* of the company. Does management appear to have a definite *plan*? This is most important because a plan is absolutely essential to success, and a good plan requires *projections*.

KEY #12: *Projections*

Projections made by management can be very illuminating. Somewhere in the management's philosophy, when explaining the future potential of their big gamble situation, they must finally bring their theories and ideas down to a discussion of *profits*. This demands that they make future projections. Be alert for specific targets, both in sales and earnings, e.g., "In the next three years it is thought that the big gamble project will generate sales of $25 million and net earnings of approximately $5 million. This is estimated to change the current net earnings from $.50 to $3.00." Here is a specific projection of sales, profits and net earnings expected in a specific time period. This piece of information is worth its weight in gold to an investor from two standpoints. First, it tells you, if the project is successful, the net earnings *will possibly* change by 600%. This is a high percentage change and it is doubtful that the price of the stock will remain unchanged. Any company that *might even be capable* of such change demands an investor's complete scrutiny.

Secondly, these projections establish rates of change that can be used as guideposts when the future quarterly earnings are reported, thus allowing the investor to establish whether the earlier projections are moving ahead or behind schedule. Should the rates of increase not live up to expectation, then it can be detected. On the other hand, earnings may be accelerated ahead of projections, a most happy sequence. Have you ever wondered, after reading an apparently outstanding quarterly earnings report, why the price of the stock drops abruptly? The answer may be that while the earnings on the surface were outstanding, they were running behind earlier projections.

Be cautious of vague, general projections which *assume* that the potential is so obvious that the management should not have to make specific projections, for example, such vagueness as "potential unlimited," or "everyone a potential prospect," or "too enormous to calculate." These nice little phrases in most cases cover up the foggy thinking of management without a specific plan. Stockholders should pin down such statements by saying, "Look, Mr. President, I have my money invested in

this project and I want to know *how much profit* and *when."*
The best management will not have to be asked this question.

KEY #13: *Profits*

It should always be kept in mind that profits and *big profits*
are what create a dynamic growth stock. In days gone by, no
discussion of profits would have been required as it was axio-
matic to any investment consideration. But today, in the era of
socialism, it becomes necessary because there are more and
more companies whose profits are directly or indirectly con-
trolled by the Government. In most cases, these companies will
never qualify for dynamic growth potential. But many investors
are often confused by the awarding of government contracts
which on the surface appear to have tremendous potential for
the company. Unfortunately, but true, in recent years, the Government has awarded contracts for some political or social
reasons, not for proficiency. This may mean the survival of these
companies and, in turn, many immediate jobs—but it does *not*
necessarily mean *profits* to the stockholders.

KEY #14: *Financial Backers*

In cases where the company is borrowing substantial amounts
of money to finance their big gamble project, it is worth while
knowing who the backers are. It must be assumed in this con-
text that if some large institutions such as banks, insurance
companies, or even wealthy private individuals, are willing to
loan their money to the company, then they believe that the
project has more than a 50% chance of success. This does not
mean, however, that because some well-known names are back-
ing the project, success is guaranteed. Institutional investors
have no special crystal ball of the future and thus they assume
risks similar to the smaller private investor. As *lenders* of funds
they will assume a preferential position in case of failure and
subsequent liquidation.

The most important factor, however, is that these large investors or lenders will have conducted extensive investigations of the company, its management and its plans, prior to making any money commitment. They are in a good position to calculate the risks that they must assume, but it is only an *opinion* that the project will be successful. As the late Gianinni of the Bank of America is reported to have said, "If you don't have some losses, you haven't taken enough risks."

Always keep in mind the four basic areas where dynamic growth is likely to occur. Searching more deeply for the keys mentioned above should help investors to focus their attention in the right direction and to *recognize* a situation when they find one. The oral contraceptive and the important developments by a little company called Syntex first came to my attention in a small science magazine. Did I know at that early time that Syntex would prove to be the big winner in the early time that Syntex would prove to be the big winner in the oral contraceptive race? Absolutely not, but the ingredients were there:

1. The stock was in a strong relative strength uptrend.
2. The idea of oral contraceptives had world-wide implications and potential.
3. The company had basic patent rights to a particular method of contraception.
4. The company was relatively small in size and had insignificant earnings to date.
5. If the oral contraceptive was successful, it should have a lasting market.

With these ingredients present, the next step is to buy stock, maybe only a small amount, but enough so that you will get the stockholders reports and begin to follow the price movement regularly. Next, develop a file about the company and also, where possible, about the industry. When you have gathered enough information to give you some confidence that the company is a definite candidate for dynamic growth, and after having watched the price action for several weeks or months, buy a significant position in the stock. When it is actually beginning to show results in terms of concrete profits, buy more and continue to add to your position during the next 100% rise.

In an earlier blueprint it was recommended that with investment grade stocks you should phase into one-third of your desired total position at a time, but with dynamic growth issues this should be divided into not more than 10% to 20% at a time; the reason is that these companies have many more uncertainties and it pays to buy into them slowly but steadily as their products prove to be successful. In this fashion, only a small percentage of your funds are risked in the very early stages, but this is of secondary consideration as these stocks have far greater potential, if correct, than the typical investment grade issue.

After a dynamic growth issue has obtained its first 100% rise it will typically consolidate and you can expect its first important reaction or slowdown. This occurs because the early speculators cannot resist the temptation to tie down at least part of this handsome profit. This may cause a 50% dip or retracement from the high point. You might wonder why I recommend continued buying through the first 100% rise; why not wait for this 50% reaction? The answer is that you don't know from what level this reaction may begin. It may be after the stock is already up 300%, and as such, a 50% dip would still leave you with a good cushion of profit.

Thus far, in our discussion of dynamic growth stocks, no thoughts on the general market and groups have been put forth. This is true simply because stocks capable of this much change are not likely to move in accord with a particular group or to be much affected by the general market. At worst, a falling general market is likely only to slow down the upward movement of such dynamic issues. Any little rally or rise in the general movement of stocks is likely to see these issues shooting into new high ground. Group considerations would follow about the same pattern, though I believe that most issues having dynamic characteristics fall into a "special situation" classification.

A way of finding the big winner is to keep a constant watch on both listed and Over-the-Counter stocks, with special emphasis on the latter which have gone up 100% or more in the past year or have substantially outperformed the average stock's gain. This can best be done by a weekly review of the tables in Barron's and making a list of all stocks that show a 100% rise during the year and are selling close to their high prices. Keep a list of these issues from week to week, and then, making a rapid fundamental appraisal of each should tell you whether they have some of the keys that go into the making of a dynamic issue. If so, then further investigation is required, but don't expect to read that this stock is a dynamic growth issue that is destined to go up at least 500%. Unfortunately, it doesn't work that way. More typically, you will have to use your own judgment as to the possible success of the situation.

Be cautious about the off-hand comments or criticisms of friends, associates or brokers. If the issue is not General Motors or American Telephone or some well-known stock, they may automatically reject it just because they have never heard of it. With a broker, he may have heard of it and that's all; he will hate to admit to you that he really doesn't know a thing about the situation, and thus will say, off-the-cuff, so to speak, "Yes, that sounds like an interesting situation" and then go on to tell you about his own "pet" of the moment. This is really not so unusual after all; even the best broker can only know about a relatively few issues and if you come up with an unknown one, he should not be expected to know much about it. The important thing is to get him to do some digging for you and to send you as much information as possible. Keep an eye on the last page of the Wall Street Journal in the market comment section;

here often are listed reports on particular stocks, along with the firm publishing the reports. Most firms will send the report to you for the asking. Be sure to buy at least a few shares and *hold these stock certificates yourself*, not in the broker's account. In this manner, all items published by the company will be mailed directly to you.

Begin your buying slowly and buy more only on a scale up. Do *not* scale down. Remember you are dealing with a highly speculative situation that has not as yet stood the test of time and may in fact be bankrupt within a few years. Regardless of how good the situation looks, or how excited you may get, sit down and decide how much money you want invested in a high risk situation and then divide the total into five or ten parts and buy on a 10% to 20% scale up. Believe me, this will keep you out of a lot of trouble. If your appraisal proves to be wrong, and it may about 75% of the time with these issues, then your losses will be held to a small percentage of your total funds and the bulk of your funds will remain free to try again with another issue. A stop loss, mentally or actually, 15% to 25% below the purchase price is recommended.

You may be asking whether, with a batting average of only 25%, this blueprint is really worth following. My answer is an unequivocal yes, for certain types of investors. It requires time to conduct investigations. It requires the ability to deal with many unknown and unproven factors. It requires the ability to make a decision, without much help from others, and it requires the ability to take many small losses. This last factor is a lot easier said than done. Some investors start this plan and immediately suffer several 15% losses. They will begin to feel that they can't make money taking losses. They also begin to get impatient when the bulk of their funds remain idle as the search for the big winner goes on. Sometimes they will "freeze" when it comes time to make another disagreeable decision about taking another loss. Their natural tendency is to become discouraged or to say the heck with it and try real estate. All this is par for the psychological warm-up for when the big one comes in.

Then things may begin to happen fast and you suddenly have a profit big enough for the second scale-up purchase when you've barely finished paying for the first purchase. And, again, as you write out the check for the second purchase, it is time to make the third. All this action should please you greatly, but quite the contrary is more typical, for things begin to happen *too* fast. You begin to doubt that buying at these advanced prices makes sense because you could have bought it just a few weeks back for half the price. The feeling that the top must be just around the corner creeps into your thinking. Having taken several small losses, you are now "profit hungry" and the emotional desire to "take a profit" gets bigger and bigger with each point price advance. Sticking to your plan is very difficult, but if you do, you may be on the way to 500% profit or more during the next two years.

While we have set a minimum of 500% appreciation in approximately two years as a guide, this was done primarily to eliminate the lessor contenders, *not* as a goal for profit-taking. I believe it can be accurately stated that any issue capable of this minimum objective may in fact be just getting up a head of steam for many years of outstanding growth. The plain facts of life are that Xerox Corp. went up more than 10,000% in less than ten years. Admittedly this is an outstanding example and one that you are not likely to duplicate easily, but it is equally true that in most every ten year period we have a handful of stocks that will go up 3,000% to 5,000% (see chart of Eckerd (Jack) on P. 155).

Knowing the basic ingredients of what to look for is the first step, buying on a scale-up basis is the second step, and patient holding of positions showing excellent profits is the third step. The bigger the profit, the less anxious you should become to sell it. Certainly the day is likely to arrive when you should be selling, but your greatest safety is a large cushion of profit. Thus give these issues plenty of time. Be sure the trend has *clearly* reversed or the percentage dip is definitely abnormally large before selling. Seek a definite fundamental reason for selling. If, after an exhaustive search, you find no reasons and the weakness can be explained by a general market downswing, then your decision should be to hold tight and appraise the next rally that occurs. If the rally rebounds with great speed and moves into new high ground by 10% or more, then you must assume that the trend is still up and no action is required.

If the rally rebounds only 75% of the way back and then stops and moves sideways or falls back, selling part of the position is advised, up to 50%. If the rally only retraces 50% or less of the decline and then begins to fall back, definite stop losses should be placed on the entire position. I cannot emphasize strongly enough, however, taking plenty of time, several months or even a year or more, to be sure that the stock is not just consolidating its recent sharp advance, allowing the earnings to catch up with the price. This can occur only, however, where a profit of 100% at a minimum has already been established on the entire position.

Traditionally high P/E ratios are of little help as a guide for selling these issues because of insufficient market seasoning. In most instances, stocks with this exceptional potential will sell at what appears to be astronomically high P/E ratios. Stocks with high ratios should be closely checked as possible dynamic growth candidates.

Many persons attempt this dynamic growth plan only to find that they are not emotionally suited for it. Others will find it fits their goals to perfection. In any case, I advise taking a fixed sum of your investment funds, possibly 25% of your total and no more than 50% to get started with. Earmark these funds for dynamic growth issues, beginning with the steps I have covered in this chapter. It will probably take three to five years before you can make a positive decision as to whether this approach is for you. If so, you will probably commit the remainder of your funds to this blueprint. If not, you may decide on a less dynamic and less emotional plan and the sooner you learn this about yourself, the faster you will select the plan that you will use for the remainder of your investment career.

Chapter XII

THE TOP TEN INDUSTRY GROUPS BLUEPRINT

The Top Ten Industry Groups blueprint is one of the most satisfactory plans for the majority of investors seeking a combination of good growth, medium to high quality stocks, and some dividend return. This plan is best suited for most investors in that they want and seek stocks that are going to show progress during each time period. I have known few private investors who truly want to buy a stock and then want it to go sideways for a year or so before it makes any significant move higher. The only investors desirous of a sideways movement lasting for some time are those who want to accumulate large quantities of a stock and it takes a long sideways movement at depressed prices for them to buy significant quantities. Once they have their positions, they also want to see some "action"— to the upside.

Now the majority of people reading this book do not have the problem of investing millions and thus have no real need for a dormant or sideways period of time. As a matter of practice, the majority of investors I have had contact with will become disgusted with a stock if it doesn't show some progress within a matter of months, and should a year or so pass they will sell out and shift their funds to other areas where the potential looks better. Some people will call this type of person a "trader" and to a degree they are right, but I believe that I can safely state that a great number of investors will follow the above pattern, unless they have some personal reason for holding the stock. For example, a person working for a company may have inside knowledge about potential developments within the company that are likely to eventually make the stock considerably higher in price.

Many investors have come to accept the fact that buying into a stock close to its bottom usually requires sitting without any progress for several years. This is not what most of them want, however, even though it is usually what they get. What the majority of investors *want* is to buy a stock and within a few weeks—better yet, days—to have it show a small profit, and within six months or so have a large profit, maybe 50% to 100% or more.

The top ten industry groups plan is designed to accomplish just such a program. It requires, like most of the other plans, one essential prerequisite which is to completely give up any and all desire to ever buy a stock at its bottom. This is essentially the "buy high, sell higher" plan and further requires the ability to buy into stocks even after they have already moved up 30% to 50% in price. If you can cope with these essential prerequisites, then the top ten industry groups plan is a most satisfactory blueprint.

As the name implies, the top ten industry groups plan seeks to keep funds invested in the leading industry groups at all times. It becomes not only a desire of this plan, but an absolute rule that the funds are concentrated in the top 10% of all groups. Again, relative strength measurements are used to determine which are the leading groups in any given time period. If fifty groups are rated, then the funds are concentrated in the top five industries; if eighty groups are rated, then the top eight. The mathematical computation of group strength, while not difficult, does require considerable time. I strongly recommend that you subscribe or have your broker—if he doesn't already—subscribe to one of the several fine services that make relative strength group tabulations weekly.

You might think at first that this approach is going to have you jumping all over the place as these groups rotate around, and while this plan does require more shifting to keep in step, it may surprise you that you may only make a few significant changes approximately two or three times a year. On Page 178 is a chart showing the rotation of industry groups from 1962 through 1965. A detailed study of this chart should be made. Note that you may shift only one or two issues or all at a time to keep your funds concentrated where the greatest potential is likely to occur. This in turn should produce the fastest profits; the bigger the cushion of profit, the greater the safety of the original principal. This is the reasoning behind the top ten industry groups approach: the strongest go up the fastest in a rising market and are the last to come down in a falling market. It should be obvious why this plan is appealing to many investors.

The first step is to determine what the leading industries are at any given point in time. Next, it should be determined how long these groups have been leading. Strangely, once into a leading position, the minimum time there is approximately six months and the longest time approximately two years, with many groups lasting for one year to 18 months. This has coincided nicely with tax considerations discussed earlier and probably accounts for the divisor of six as an element in the above periods of time. This means that approximately twice per year some rotation in the leading groups is likely to occur and this plan requires that you shift with the strength. As this rotation tends to occur in conjunction with an intermediate general market dip, it becomes extremely important to watch and buy into the new strength that develops on the upswing following the intermediate market dip.

Assuming this plan is started after the next intermediate market dip, it will require 30 to 45 calendar days past the intermediate bottom day to clearly determine what this new leadership will be. Buying into these areas as soon as a clear decision

Rotation of Top Ten Industry Groups 1962-1965

1962

Group	J	F	M	A	M	J	J	A	S	O	N	D
Aircraft	9	8										
Airlines				4	1	1	1	2	2			6
Aluminum												
Amusement												
Auto	6	1	1	4	2	3	6	3	2	2	1	1
Auto Equip.												
Baking												
Banking	4	10						8	8	10		
Build. Mat.												
Business Mach.	2	8	9	7								
Cement					8	6						
Chemicals	8	4	3	5	10	6	6	7	6	4	5	3
Coal												4
Container												8
Cosmetics												
Drugs												
Elec. Equip.												
Electronics												
Farm Equip.												
Finance	5	5	5	6	8	9		10	5	5	10	
Food	7	6		8	9					9		
Food Chains	9	7										
Glass			2	9								
Gold	1	8	9	7	7	7	9	9	4			
Insurance	1	2	2	1	1							

1963

Group	J	F	M	A	M	J	J	A	S	O	N	D
Aircraft												
Airlines	7	2	2	2	1	1	1	1	2	2	1	1
Auto	1	1	1	2	2	2	4	2	1	1	2	4
Banking	7	7	7									
Business Mach.								4	4	2	2	
Cement												
Chemicals	8	9	8	5	7	9			7	5	4	4
Drugs									3	5		
Farm Equip.	10	9	4	5	9	10		8	8			
Glass												
Gold	4	3	3	1	7	8		7		8		

1964

Group	J	F	M	A	M	J	J	A	S	O	N	D
Airlines	1	1	1	1	1	1	2	6		1	1	1
Auto								8	6	9		
Business Mach.	2	3	8	6		4	8					
Chemicals	6	9	8	9								
Drugs	8	5	10				6	6	8			
Farm Equip.	9	10	5	4	2	3	1	1	1	1	1	3
Glass					8	9	10					

1965

Group	J	F	M	A	M	J	J	A	S	O	N	D
Airlines	10	4					5	1	1	1		
Auto	9											
Business Mach.								5	8	7		
Drugs	6	5	4	8	7	9	9	8	10	6	5	6
Farm Equip.		8	7	7	8	4	3	3	3	4		
Glass								3	8			

Investment.
Liquor
Machinery
Mach. Tool
Meat Pack.
Metal Fab.
Min. & Smelt.
Motion Pic.
Natural Gas
Oil
Paper
Publ. & Edu.
Radio-TV
Rails
Rail Equip.
Retail Merch.
Rubber
Science
Soft Drink
Steel
Textile
Tobacco
Utilities
Variety
Vend. Mach.

1965 1964 1963 1962

Group data obtained from Investors Research Company, 924 Laguna St., Santa Barbara, Calif.
Illustrations by E. S. Jensen.

has been made is essential. It is possible and very probable that one or two groups that were leaders in the time preceding the dip will continue to show power. Be a little slower about new buying into these groups, but definitely buy them if they still show strength. The odds favor that, having bought into groups emerging as leaders 30 to 45 days *past* an intermediate bottom, they will remain leaders for the six month period following the bottom.

Roughly four to six months later, another dip is due and again some rotation can be expected. During the first couple of weeks of this next dip, the odds are good that these leading groups will continue to make new highs. As a market dip worsens, it will begin to take its toll on the leading groups also. A decision to sell and raise cash for the next bottom can be made, or a decision to hold through to determine the damage caused and to see if the groups will again remain strong on the other side of the dip. To sell or ride the dip is always a difficult decision, but the best answer depends, to a large degree, on the cushion of profit built up during the previous rise. If your profit is 50% or more, the odds favor you can ride most any intermediate break (barring a major collapse) and still show a good profit even if the group fails to remain among the leaders. If your profit is 25% or less, it is usually advisable to sell, as a break may put you in a loss position.

If you have little or no profit, or a loss, and you expect further market declines, sell without reservation. The loss is likely to just get bigger. It would be nice to assume that all of your stocks showed a 50% plus profit which is not totally unrealistic following this blueprint; then your decision may be to ride out the dip and see what happens. What is likely to happen is that most all of your stocks will decline 10% to 30% from their high points and will bottom approximately the same time as the general market does. These stocks, however, are likely to be the ones that will *bounce the best*; thus when the definite downward market pressure subsides and the Dow Jones Industrial

Average is still mushing around, your stocks are likely to stage a strong rally, recovering at least half to all of the amount lost during the decline.

It is extremely important to appraise this rally as it is the key to your immediate actions. The stocks that bounce the fastest and the strongest, actually breaking into new high ground, are likely to remain leaders for the next time period. Those that rally the slowest and the least, percentage-wise, are likely candidates for sale, not necessarily because they are about to fall again in price, but more likely because they will be passed up by emerging strong groups, and this plan *demands* that you shift into these new groups as soon as this determination can be positively made.

Once a decision to shift to another group is made, the next decision is what stock within the group to purchase. There are several possibilities:

1. The quality leader.
2. The relative strength leader.
3. The biggest dividend payer.
4. A likely "catch-up" candidate.

Quality Leader

By the time a group ranks in the top 10%, the highest quality stock within the group should be in a very definite relative strength uptrend. Surprisingly, these stocks may not necessarily be too far off their recent lows. Buying into these quality leader stocks within each group is strictly a matter of preference by individual investors and is primarily a psychological desire to own generally recognized leading companies with historical records of good earnings. It is *not* necessarily the desire to find the individual stock likely to appreciate the most during the group move. The quality leader may do well, but it is unlikely—though possible—to be the appreciation leader of the swing.

Relative Strength Leader

The relative strength leader is the stock that typically leads the rise in the group from its beginning. This one is likely to have the greatest appreciation from its bottom to wherever the top may eventually prove to be. It should also be viewed as the possible *crystal ball* for the balance of the group. Buying into this stock after its group finally gets into the leading 10% of groups can be one of the surest ways to make good profits in a relatively short time period. By the time the group hits the top ten, the relative strength leader may have just been warming up to what is to come. Now add the plus factor of group recognition or enthusiasm and this stock will typically begin to move *faster*. Assume that this issue has risen 50% to 100% during a year's period, prior to the groups hitting the top ten; it should now move the next 100% in approximately half that time. There is nothing hard and fast about this last concept but it has a batting average above 50%. What does occur that confuses these timing considerations is that the relative strength leader, having appreciated the most, often times will go dormant or sideways for several months, shortly after the group has reached this top ten phase. This is because the catch-ups are beginning to move and money may in fact be flowing out of the relative strength leader and into those dragging behind.

Thus, for a while, the original relative strength leader may appear to have topped out, or at least to be dead in the water. But the reasons for this company's being so strong may be that it has made the greater profitability advances within that particular field. As such, after several months of consolidation, this stock is likely to take off again. Now, while I have stated that this relative strength leader is the one likely to appreciate the most percentage-wise from its bottom to the top of its swing, I have not stated that it is the candidate likely to make you, as an investor, the most money.

Timing your purchase of the relative strength leader is often difficult. First of all, at the absolute *bottom*, the stock and group are in downtrends. Buying into an issue under these circumstances would violate every principle I have set forth in this book thus far, and at best would be termed a *"guess,"* not an investment calculation. In the very early stages of the relative strength leader's uptrend, it is always suspect because it has no support or confirmation from other stocks within the industry. Thus, for the moment, it becomes a black sheep. As its trend continues to advance, and finally the group begins to show signs of life, the stock has advanced considerably in price. Thus, while from an historical standpoint, it typically goes up the most from bottom to top, it has often proven more advantageous, percentage-wise, for investors to buy a *catch-up* candidate.

Biggest Dividend Payer

Conclusions similar to those drawn for the quality leader apply when purchasing the stocks paying the largest dividend within the group. As described in the chapter on income objectives, appreciation is of secondary importance to stability and high yield. The difference in buying these stocks when the group has entered the top 10% is that, unlike the quality leader, these stocks in all likelihood are not in definite relative strength uptrends, but are likely to be in sideways consolidation and still have a better than average yield. Because the factors affecting the particular industry are likely to eventually affect all the stocks within the industry, the big dividend payer becomes almost a doubly safe situation at this point. Its large dividend makes it less vulnerable to downside risk, and the improving industry factors are apt to create a greater demand for the issue. Under these conditions, it is often possible to buy the biggest dividend payer and also get some appreciation within a relatively short time. The amount of this appreciation is unlikely to equal that of the leader growth stocks discussed earlier, or the relative strength leader, or some catch-up candidate to be discussed below. In fact, however, the big dividend payers are one type of catch-up stocks.

Catch-Up Candidates

As the name implies, any stock exclusive of the relative strength leader is in fact some type of a catch-up situation. In actual practice, however, while only one stock may be the prime relative strength leader in the very early stages, it is not usually very long before one or more other stocks in the group will begin to move. In the very early stages of the move, these generally will not grow as fast as the prime leader, and because of this it pays to buy the prime leader. By the time a group is in the top ten, somewhere between 50% and 75% of all the stocks within the group have made some definite progress. The remaining 25% or more form the true catch-up candidates for this approach. Often these issues may be still declining. More often, however, they are moving sideways in a relatively narrow consolidation zone. Because this zone is fairly easy to define, and because no upside potential as yet has been used up, these stocks many times will prove to be some of the best candidates for eventual percentage gains within the group.

If the advent of the jet plane was going to have profound effect on the entire airline industry, then those companies who were first to recognize it were likely to be among the early winners. But the total effect was that eventually the entire industry would show a change as they, too, began to purchase jet aircraft, and this would continue right down to the last little feeder line.

Thus when a group first gains top ten status, there usually are several good catch-up candidates that may be purchased that will produce outstanding capital appreciation. Many times a lesser-known company in a catch-up phase will produce the greatest percentage gains. A list of potential catch-up candidates should be made when the group enters this top ten status. Buying should be postponed until the first positive signs of upward thrust in price—usually a price breakout or unusually big volume. In buying catch-up candidates, the prime consideration is price appreciation, and as such, the factor of quality becomes one of individual preference. In most instances, however, *lower priced* catch-up stocks will show greater percentage gains.

The top ten industry groups blueprint is the plan I recommend to the vast majority of private investors because it may be utilized in several different ways. It allows the investor to deal within a specific individual group with either the highest quality stock, the large dividend payer, or the speculative issues. It at all times maximizes probabilities in the investor's favor by having favorable group psychology, which is extremely important but often ignored. The majority of the stocks selected under this blueprint will be companies of good quality or at least ones where the product or service has stood the test of time. This is the big difference between this plan and the dynamic growth plan. This plan requires more shifting, particularly in the beginning phase, than some of the other plans, but with commissions averaging less than 1% to buy and 1% to sell, this is a small price to pay to insure that your total funds are always working the hardest by maximizing the probabilities.

The selling technique involved in an individual issue is similar to the procedure discussed in an earlier chapter. If traditionally high P/E valuations have been attained and the group continues in the top 10%, the rotation down to a catch-up candidate will prove worthwhile. The key factor here is that if the group should become weak, yet an individual stock remains strong, stop loss orders are recommended. From time to time a group will turn weak causing you to sell, only to again become strong, requiring your re-purchase, possibly at higher prices. All these factors have been considered when making a recommendation that this approach is the one best suited for the majority of investors.

A great part of shifting or switching errors can be eliminated if purchases are geared to intermediate general market dips, and by making new commitments during the 30 to 45 days past these bottoms as emerging strength creates new groups as candidates and also determines if previous groups should continue to be held. In this fashion, the 30 to 60 day period past each intermediate bottom (which, remember, occurs approximately two and a half times per year or five times in two years) is the point of maximum action for this plan. This has the investor typically selling out of groups which turn weak on a rally, and buying into groups and stocks showing powerful thrust strength, a combination of factors that is hard to beat.

Chapter XIII

THE AGE OF THE COMPUTER

In late 1963, the president of one of the leading statistical stock market services called me and informed me that he had just completed making the final tape of all relevant stock data for all stocks on the New York Stock Exchange and the American Stock Exchange for computer use. His data went back to 1960 and he stated his belief that his firm, if not the first, was certainly among the first to have compilation completed. I was most flattered when he asked me what he should do with these tapes. My answer then, as it would be now, is to find the men who know "how to play the tune." There were not many men then and only a few more today who would know how to program a computer in order to make it a worthwhile investment tool.

From that day in 1963 to the present, however, the adaptation of computers into the investment field has occurred with amazing speed in a field which is typically slow to change. Most of this computer activity has been concentrated in the large institutional type research departments. The exact effect the introduction of the computer will have on stock market dealing is just beginning to unfold. I do not believe it will greatly alter the majority of ideas and concepts expressed in this book, and my reasons are simply that the concepts I have expressed are boiled down in the final analysis to people. It is still people who create the supply-demand factors that make prices rise or fall.

Beyond this, however, it would appear that *time* considerations may be changing rapidly. In the past a research department decision to purchase an issue tended to be a long drawn-out affair. It started possibly with a junior analyst doing a complete and thorough research report on a particular industry or stock. This he passed on to his department head for review and further discussion and research. If the second look still appeared favorable, the information was moved on to the senior analyst for a decision. At this level, the senior analyst usually would arrange for an interview with the company management and finally prepare the report that is sent to clients advising purchase or sale. This process was typically slow and thus was reflected by relatively slow stock price movement.

Today, however, the vast majority of the historical data is only the press of a button away. The ability to survey all listed stocks rapidly and to feed the new daily data for comparison into a computer allows for rapid detection of unusual activity or change in the norm. Today, in practice, once something unusual is detected, it is possible for a senior analyst to depart by jet and interview management, see at first hand new products and developments and still return to his office that evening. The next morning his findings may be passed on to the investment community or large individual clients. In either case, the result is the same: a tremendous speedup rate of decision making in regard to buying or selling. This is likely to be reflected in individual stock movement by an acceleration of trends. On the first day the computer says BUY, some purchases will be made on the computer recommendation only, but any quantity of buying will be detected easily by others who in turn will not be far behind with their purchases. The result could be a chain reaction, developing considerable thrust in the early stage of a new trend. Stocks may literally "fly" by moving virtually straight up. When the trend comes to an end and the computer registers SELL, equally swift drops may occur.

These short fast shifts in trends may not be welcomed by all investors, but should they come to pass, it will only make the importance of group movement, relative strength, trends, and many of the axioms of the market (e.g., buy late, sell early) more important than ever before in order to continue on the profit side. Like it or not, the computer has become a fact of life in the stock market and it is almost sure to have great effect in this century. Failure to recognize this change may cost you your fortune; get in step with it and it may help you to make your fortune.

THE END

"Well done is better than well said."

Benjamin Franklin

SOURCES OF STOCK MARKET INFORMATION

STOCK MARKET INDICATORS

Indicator Digest, Inc.:

Palisades Park, New Jersey 07650. A composite indicator approach with periodic chart display of individual indicators. A trial subscription is available.

FUNDAMENTAL INFORMATION

Moody's Investors Service, Inc.:

99 Church St., New York, N. Y. 10007. "Industrial Manual," "Bank and Finance Manual," "Transportation Manual." This outstanding service comes in large hard-bound volumes for industrial, transportation and utilities and is published yearly. A concise and complete historical background of companies is presented. A supplemental service keeps data current between publications. This service may be found in many brokerage offices. It covers many companies not covered by other services and is one of the most complete sources of fundamental information.

Standard & Poor's Corp.:

345 Hudson St., New York, N. Y. 10014 "Standard & Poor's Listed Stock Reports." A single page presentation of (1) companies' activities, background and recent developments, (2) a 10-year financial data report including sales, operating costs,

taxes, various ratios, earnings and dividends. A recent new addition has been the inclusion of the yearly high and low price/earnings ratios for 10 years. (3) Capitalization and stockholder information.

Without doubt, this service is one of the most widely used as a rapid source of information concerning individual companies. Many brokerage firms will send a Standard & Poor's report on a particular company without charge. While the information is condensed, it also appears very complete.

The Value Line Investment Survey:

5 East 44th St., New York, N. Y. 10017. Another excellent source of background and current information about particular companies.

TECHNICAL CHART INFORMATION

CHARTS — MONTHLY

Securities Research Company:

A Division of United Business Service Co., 208 Newbury St., Boston, Mass. 02116. "Cycli-Graphs" cover 12 years of price, earnings, volume, dividends and relative strength. I believe this to be the outstanding chart service in the country today. The majority of graphs presented in this book are taken from this service. Its value lies in the fact that it covers 12 years of information in one small graph. Statistically, it would require volumes of pages to record the same information. Published quarterly; plotted monthly on a semi-logarithmic scale.

CHARTS — WEEKLY

Securities Research Company:

A Division of United Business Service Co., 208 Newbury St., Boston, Mass. 02116. "Security Charts" cover approximately a 20 months period of price, earnings, dividends, volume and relative strength (Ratio-cator). Published monthly; plotted weekly on a semi-logarithmic scale.

Trendlines:

345 Hudson St., New York, N. Y. 10014. "Current Market Perspectives." Arithmetical graphs plotted weekly. Broken into groups. Gives the traditionally high and low price/earnings ratios. Published monthly.

R. W. Mansfield Co.:

26 Journal Square, Jersey City, N. J. 07306. This is another outstanding chart service displaying a vast amount of data. A detailed description may be obtained by sending for a trial subscription.

CHARTS — DAILY

Trendlines:

345 Hudson St., New York, N. Y. 10014. "Daily Basis Stock Charts." Arithmetical scale charts plotted daily and displaying the price, volume and 200-day moving average. Also a statistical insert giving earnings and dividend information. Published weekly.

SPECIAL NOTE:

THE AUTHOR HAS PRESENTED THE ABOVE *SOURCES OF STOCK MARKET INFORMATION* IN THE HOPE OF AIDING INVESTORS IN THEIR SEARCH FOR INFORMATION. MANY OF THE ABOVE SERVICES WILL MAKE SPECIFIC RECOMMENDATIONS FOR THE PURCHASE OR SALE OF INDIVIDUAL SECURITIES. THE AUTHOR IS IN NO WAY ENDORSING THE EDITORIAL OPINIONS OR THE RECOMMENDATIONS OF THESE SERVICES.